Tampering with Truth

The New Left in the Lord's Church

David W. Hester

Publishing Designs, Inc.
Huntsville, Alabama

Publishing Designs, Inc.
P.O. Box 3241
Huntsville, Alabama 35810

David W. Hester
dwhest@bellsouth.net

David W. Hester

All Scripture quotations, unless otherwise noted, are
from the King James Version of the Bible.

Printed in the United States of America

Library of Congress Cataloging-in-Publication Data

Hester, David W. (David Wayne), 1965-
  Tampering with truth : the New Left in the Lord's church / David Hester.
    p. cm.
  ISBN 978-0-929540-65-8 (alk. paper)
  1. Liberalism (Religion) 2. Theology. I. Title.
  BR1617.H47 2007
  286.6'3—dc22

                    2007000023

Contents

Introduction

The Lord's church is in the midst of its most serious division in a hundred years. Interestingly, while technology and mass communication have made tremendous advances, the division in 1906 with the Christian Church, and the current division are quite similar. A small but determined cadre of highly educated preachers and academics has pressed for radical change in congregations across the country. Gaining control of key papers and schools, these individuals have succeeded, to a certain extent, in getting their message out and making it stick in the minds of unsuspecting brethren. After gathering a sizable number of supporters, they then push the leadership of the congregation to change to meet their wishes—or face the prospect of division. In the meantime, the leaders of the movement speak in somber tones of their "extremist" past, how it supposedly mirrors the "sad, sad history" of churches of Christ, and how they are making a clean break with "sectarianism" to experience "spiritual freedom," the "refreshing breezes of the Spirit." In so doing, the church is divided and the Lord Himself is persecuted again.

In 1994 I wrote concerning these matters. *Among the Scholars* was my attempt to put into writing what I perceived then to be a serious challenge to the purity and unity of the body of Christ. I was not alone; others penned books and articles warning about the same danger, but approaching it from different angles. Our warnings did not go unheeded; brethren across the country listened to what we said, and in many cases took action to either prevent the danger from reaching their congregations, or else took a firm stand against error already present. However, the division that many feared would take place inevitably happened in too many areas.

The thesis of *Among the Scholars* was twofold: first, the leaders of the "New Left" largely came from the 1960s and retained the same destructive radicalism of the political leaders of their generation. Second, many of them also came from the "anti" wing of the brotherhood and retained the same divisive spirit, while rejecting their former beliefs. This was based more on a gut feeling, rooted in the speeches and writings of some of them. In the intervening years, much more has been said and written by the leaders of the New Left, which make their motivations even clearer. These statements and assertions beg to be examined in light of Scripture.

A Web site of a church in central Alabama is a case in point. This church resulted from a division of a well-established, doctrinally sound congregation. On its home page you may read these words:

> Our congregation is a beautiful blend of previously unchurched folks and of Christians from varying religious backgrounds, including Church of Christ, Free Will and Southern Baptist, Methodist, Pentecostal, and Catholic. Each of us decided that it was time for a body of believers to come together and focus on the core tenets of the Christian faith without regard to denominational traditions and rituals that for too long have divided God's people.[1]

While at first blush such may seem innocuous, when one examines the site he immediately sees the meaning. This is nothing less than a call for open fellowship with all denominations. When one considers that this particular church has divided yet again, and that one of its former leaders has left churches of Christ altogether and has led a division in a denominational church, he sees the bitter fruit of drinking deeply from poisoned wells.

Consider also a Web site calling for "gender justice" among churches of Christ. On its home page, one can read this definition of the term:

> In general, gender justice means recognizing that men and women are created by God, redeemed by Christ, and gifted by the Spirit truly without distinction or partiality. In Christian community, gender justice means encouraging both men and women to exercise their Spirit-given gifts in the church's work, worship, and leadership,

---

1. http://www.crossviewchurch.com/home.html.

and celebrating the truth that the Spirit grants such gifts without respect to gender. *Concretely, gender justice in the Church of Christ includes opening traditionally masculine leadership roles and activities (deacon, elder, minister, worship leader, preacher, teacher, etc.) to women,* and encouraging men to discover and cultivate their gifts for activities traditionally performed by women[2] (emphasis added-dh).

One of the links to this site is to the Cahaba Valley Church of Christ in Birmingham, Alabama. Billing itself as "an Ecumenical Church of Christ," the leaders make it clear where they are:

> One of the ways that we as a congregation have been challenged to live up to the mandate to follow the call of God is to allow God to change tradition. In the churches that most of us grew up in, it was assumed that women would never take a part in leading public worship. At the same time, it has become increasingly clear that cultural bias against women in general has often been a major factor in how both human culture and the church as well have talked about women and their ministries as disciples.

> By 1984 we increasingly sensed God leading us to trust the work of the Spirit of Christ in individual believers, male and female, to live out the ministries inspired by the spiritual gifts that he grants to each believer. As a result, we began to have serious conversations about whether our practice of allowing only men to pray, serve communion, lead singing and plan worship was anchored in inherited tradition or reflected God's will. In 1988 and 1989, we carried out very detailed study of the Scriptures, and after much prayer and searching, the elders of our congregation concluded that it was the work of the Spirit to assign the roles and gifts of each person and that, therefore, women would be invited, along with the men, to seek to identify their gifts and ministries, including that of being involved in the leadership of worship. Women were not required to participate, but they would have the same freedom as men to explore and use their gifts in light of their reading of Scripture and their own faith in God. Women were then invited to volunteer along with the men of our congregation.

> As a result, women have come to participate in all aspects of our congregation's life, from leading public worship to serving as deacons and to teaching adult Bible classes.[3]

---

2. http://www.gal328.org/.
3. http://www.cahabavalley.org/history_role_of_women.htm.

If one wonders where 1 Timothy 2 factors into this, the answer is that these individuals attempt to explain away the restrictions Paul placed on the role of women. In the case of Cahaba Valley, they claim that Paul did not pen those words; rather, they say, they were written in the second century by the leaders of the church. Additionally, they claim the passage was written to accommodate the culture of the day —implying that we do not have to follow it.[4]

Max Lucado is a talented writer, and a gifted speaker. His books consistently top the best-seller lists, and he has become a nationally renowned preacher. However, Lucado is also a false teacher. Indeed, the agenda of the New Left is clearly seen when one examines some of his statements and writings. Consider what he asserted on his syndicated radio program, "Upwards":

> LUCADO: You can be sure that neither death nor life, nor angels, nor ruling spirits, nothing now, nothing in the future, no powers, nothing above us, nothing below us, nor anything else in the world will ever be able to separate us from the love of God that is in Christ Jesus. You see, in God, by virtue of your adoption, you have a divine affinity, you have eternal security, and you have a golden opportunity. I cannot imagine an orphan turning down an opportunity to be adopted. With one decision, with one raising of the hand, with one agreement to leave the orphanage, that person all of a sudden goes from being abandoned to claimed, from having no name to a new name, no future to a new future, he leaves the orphanage, and enters the house of the father.
>
> That's what God offers you. There is no quiz, no examination, no charge. All you have to do is say "yes" to the Father. And many of you have done that. But I have a hunch that not all of you have. I have a hunch that there's a few of you listening, even now, and God is using this to pull on your heart. The Holy Spirit is informing you of something that you have never really heard before—and that is, God is ready to be your Father. Maybe you never understood that the invitation was for everyone. Maybe you thought you weren't worthy. Maybe now you do understand. God will make you worthy, and the invitation is for you. And all you have to do is call him Father. Just call him Father. Just turn your heart to him even right now as I am speaking. Call him your Father. And your Father will respond. Why don't you do that?

---

4. http://www.cahabavalley.org/women's_role_study_document.htm.

[Instrumental music playing in background] "Father, I give my heart to you. I give you my sins, I give you my tears, I give you my fears, I give you my whole life. I accept the gift of your Son on the cross for my sins. And I ask you, Father, to receive me as your child. Through Jesus I pray. Amen."

ANNOUNCER: And friend, if you prayed along with Max Lucado just now, here on UPWARDS, we want to welcome you into the family of God. We hope you will contact us and share your personal testimony. If you are already a believer, we thank you for praying for these new brothers and sisters in Christ . . . Now Max Lucado returns with a special word for those who received the gift of salvation just moments ago in prayer.

LUCADO [instrumental music playing in the background]: Today is the first day you've ever prayed a prayer like that. Could you do me a favor? Could you write me a letter? I don't have anything I am going to ask from you. I do have a letter I would like to send to you. I'd like to give you a word about the next step or two. I want to encourage you to find a church, I want to encourage you to be baptized, I want to encourage you to read your Bible. *But I don't want you to do any of that so that you will be saved. I want you to do all of that because you are saved.* You see, your Father has a great life planned for you, and I want to tell you about it. Give us a call, and drop me a note. And, thanks my friend, for making the greatest decision of your life[5] (emphasis added-dh).

As stunning as this is, it's not the only time Lucado has asserted such. In 2000 Word Publishing produced a tract entitled "He Chose the Nails." In it, Lucado writes:

Would you let him save you? This is the most important decision you will ever make. Why don't you give your heart to him right now? . . . Go to God in prayer and tell him, I am a sinner in need of grace. I believe that Jesus died for me on the cross. I accept your offer of salvation. It's a simple prayer with eternal results . . .

I pray that you'll accept this great gift of salvation. Believe me, this is not only the most important decision you'll ever make, it's also the greatest decision you'll ever make. There's no higher treasure than God's gift of salvation.[6]

---

5. Max Lucado, Radio Station KJAK, Lubbock, Texas, December 1996, http://users.abilene.com/~wgoforth/Luc3.htm.

6. Lucado, *He Did This Just for You* (Nashville: Word, 2000), 50, 52.

The contrast between what Lucado asserts and what the New Testament actually teaches could not be clearer. Yet, he is not alone. Rubel Shelly asks:

> For some, salvation is an event marked by what is commonly called "the sinner's prayer." For others, the critical moment at which one is saved is marked by the waters of baptism. For still others, the defining occurrence is a life-transforming experience of the Holy Spirit. Which is it? Have you ever seen a multiple-choice question on an exam with the option: "all of the above"? Or what about this very postmodern option: "none of the above—but a relationship that grows over time"?[7]

I was a freshman at Freed-Hardeman University in 1984, when Shelly was allowed to make a statement at Open Forum in order to clarify his views on baptism, which were just then coming under scrutiny. At that time, he asserted his belief that the purpose of baptism was for salvation, and that he had not changed. He could not now make such an assertion.

In September 1993, Magnolia Church of Christ in Florence, Alabama, had a joint worship service with a Methodist church; Magnolia's preacher, Joe Van Dyke, downplayed doctrinal differences and said all churches should unite in spite of those differences. The following spring, Van Dyke delivered a sermon at Faith Tabernacle. What he said on that occasion at the close reveals much of the mind-set of the New Left.

Throughout the service, the instrument was used. Van Dyke declared they were standing "on holy ground," and that this event had "been a dream of mine for a few years." When he came to the end of his sermon, Van Dyke addressed a question that was being asked by many at the time. What if, toward the end of such a joint worship service, a man was to come forward and ask, "Men and brethren, what shall we do?" One preacher replies as did Peter in Acts 2:38, while the other preacher gives a different answer. One says baptism is immersion, while the other disagrees. What then?

In addressing the question, Van Dyke proceeded to list a number of preachers in the audience. He then said: "Don't you think that if

---

7. Rubel Shelly & John O. York, *The Jesus Proposal* (Siloam Springs, AR: Leafwood Publishers, 2003), 140.

somebody needs to respond this evening that we can all get together down here at the front and work something out that needs to be done?" The audience erupted in cheers, yells, and much applause. He then said, "We can work it out, brothers, we can work it out. If you need prayer, we can pray. If you want baptism, we can baptize. If you want—whatever it is you need tonight, there's some preacher here that can minister to you in the name of Jesus."[8]

The audacity of such an assertion is breathtaking. Think about the day of Pentecost. When those people said, "Men and brethren, what shall we do," how did Peter respond? According to Van Dyke, Peter should have said: "Well, we've got the Pharisees in the audience; we've got the Sadducees present; we've got the scribes and lawyers; we've also got the apostles. Don't you think that we can all get together on Solomon's porch and work out something that needs to be done?" How ludicrous!

We know how Peter replied: "Repent, and be baptized every one of you in the name of Jesus Christ for the remission of sins, and ye shall receive the gift of the Holy Ghost" (Acts 2:38). But Van Dyke said, "Whatever it is you need tonight, there's some preacher here that can minister to you." Peter certainly did not give that kind of invitation.

Consider what Van Dyke said at the close:

> We've got people coming to lead us in a time of response, and so I'm just going to issue the invitation. If you want to go where God wants you to go—be what God wants you to be—do what God wants you to do—without concern for who you are but concern only for who he is and where he wants you to go, if there's something missing in your life right now that you think a response in this assembly could supply, then [at that point, the music started—dh] we invite you to come right now. All of these ministers will be down here to receive you. If there's some spiritual need in your life, won't you come right now while we have some music together.[9] [At that point, the music reached a crescendo and continued—dh.]

This event was simply the culmination of what the New Left in the church wants to take place. This has been repeated many times, in

---

8. Joe Van Dyke at Faith Tabernacle, 1995, tape recording.
9. Ibid.

many places since it first happened. Those in leadership positions within the New Left have been working long and hard to make such meetings a reality. In so doing, the work of numerous brethren falls by the wayside and the cause of Christ suffers.

As we shall see in the course of this study, such positions as those taken by Lucado, Shelly, and Van Dyke affect one's views on fellowship. Given the practices of these men, it should come as no surprise that they are in open fellowship with the denominational world. How different this is from the great preachers of the past. In many cases they had come out of denominationalism and were calling on others to do the same.

This book is an attempt to shine the light of truth upon the New Left in the Lord's church. In so doing, we will enter a different world. It is one in which up is down, and down is up. Or as the great philosopher Humpty Dumpty once put it: "When I choose a word, it means what I want it to mean—nothing more, nothing less." Such seems to summarize the mind-set of the leaders of the New Left.

Each chapter is followed by discussion questions, which are designed to stimulate open conversation in a class setting.

- Chapter 1 asks, "Was Jesus a 'Scholar'?" That is, would He feel right at home among the academic Left—or would He rather speak out against it? What was His nature? How did He view Scripture? The chapter will address these concerns.

- Chapter 2, "How Shall We Interpret the Bible," looks at the nature of Scripture. Believe it or not, there are those among the Left who are questioning the inspiration and inerrancy of God's Word. In answering them, we will examine what the Bible says about itself, and how we should interpret it.

- Chapter 3, "Among the Scholars—Again," details my trip to the 1996 Christian Scholars Conference at David Lipscomb University. It was just as interesting, and enlightening, as my previous excursion to Harding in 1993.

- Chapter 4, "Reflections on Current Problems among Churches of Christ: A Proposal" is the text of what I presented on that occasion.

- Chapter 5 revisits a subject that led to a major division at the beginning of the twentieth century. "'Instrumental Music Is Not a Salvation Issue'—But We Will Have It, Regardless!" examines the trend among some large congregations to introduce instrumental music in worship—in spite of clear New Testament teaching on the matter.

- Chapter 6, "What about Contemporary 'Christian' Music?" The same congregations that introduce the instrument are also employing contemporary "Christian" music in their assemblies, and encouraging all their members to buy and listen to CDs of the same style of music. Is it safe? Close attention will be paid to it.

- Chapter 7 seems to have a strange title, at first blush: "The Holy Spirit, Pope Benedict XVI, and the New Left." How do they relate? Read the chapter and find out. The issue of how the Holy Spirit works is entwined in the agenda of the New Left. The positions the leaders take on the matter lead them into some curious conclusions. Space will be devoted to just how the Holy Spirit does work today, according to Scripture.

- Chapter 8, "Restoration or Revisionist History," carefully examines the continuing practice of Leftist historians to revise the history of churches of Christ in America. As is the case with the political Left, the leaders of the current movement within the church have a definite agenda they are pursuing.

- Chapter 9, "The Jesus Seminar," addresses an issue that is percolating within the religious world in general, and may yet affect the church in the near future—through the New Left. As will be described, the Jesus Seminar attempts to re-explain both who Jesus is and the nature of Scripture. What is currently significant is that the Left has been quiet about it. Could it be that the goals of both dovetail?

- Chapter 10 asks an unusual question: "Is Young Absalom Safe— In His Youth Group?" That is to say, can we continue to assume that all is well within youth groups in our congregations? Given the fact that too many of them are being taken to events that employ unscriptural worship and that use false teachers, the question is all too relevant.

- Chapter 11 asks, "Do We Have the Right Kind of Love?" Love is important for both the child of God and the local congregation; however, it must be the right kind. The Scriptures instruct us on the kind of love we are to cultivate; it is the case that the New Left's idea of "love" is far afield from God's Word.

- Chapter 12, "The Church Needs to Watch," is an exhortation to all Christians for renewed vigilance in all areas. God uses the analogy of a watchman in Ezekiel 3:17 and 33:7 to encourage the prophet; the principle still holds true today for all Christians. There are many areas that bear watching if the Lord's church is to be successful in its mission.

- Chapter 13 ends the book on an optimistic note. "Some Reasons for Hope" details encouraging signs within the body of Christ over the past decade. The New Left has apparently not been as successful as it would like to be in transforming the church into just another denomination. While it has made advances, evidence abounds to indicate a note of desperation among the leaders of the movement.

As we begin our journey through the maze of the New Left, we must consider the motivation at work behind its leaders. One must not forget that both the political Left and the Left of the Lord's church are strikingly similar. Thus, when one comes across the writings of former Leftist leaders of the 1960s who have since turned away from the movement, it is enlightening—simply for the fact that it also sheds some light on the Leftists within the body of Christ.

David Horowitz was a co-founder and editor of *Ramparts* magazine, a Marxist publication of the 1960s. Horowitz, along with others, was present at the inception of the political New Left, and helped to promote its agenda—opposition to the war in Vietnam, support of the Black Panther Party, and other extreme radical causes. However, in the late 1970s a series of events shook his beliefs and helped to begin a transformation. They were the communist Vietnamese government's invasion of Cambodia, and the subsequent slaughter of two million Cambodians; and the murder of a close friend of Horowitz by a Black Panther, and the lack of interest in prosecuting the crime. Consequently, in 1984 Horowitz—along with Peter Collier—issued a public statement announcing they were wrong in opposing the war in Vietnam, and called on other Leftists of that era who had "second thoughts" to do the same. For good measure, they announced their support of the re-election of Ronald Reagan—thus making their political transformation complete.

Since then, Horowitz has written a number of books further explaining his philosophical transformation and his take on current political trends—as well as his continued monitoring of his ex-friends of the Left. In 2000 he penned the book *The Politics of Bad Faith*. In it he included a letter addressed to a former mentor, Ralph Miliband, an English Marxist and author of *Parliamentary Socialism*. Notice what Horowitz says, in part:

> Our choice of politics was never a matter of partial commitments. To choose the Left was to define a way of being in the world. (For us, the personal was always political.) It was choosing a future in which human beings would finally live as they were meant to live: no longer self-alienated and divided, but equal, harmonious, and whole.
>
> Grandiose as this project was, it was not something we had invented, but the inspiration for a movement that was coterminous with modernity itself . . . This is the true self-vision of the Left: An army of saints on the march against injustice, lacking itself the capacity for evil. The Left sees its revolutions as pillars of fire that light up humanity's deserts, but burn no civilizations as they pass.[10]

Such language well describes some of those at the vanguard of the current movement within churches of Christ. Theirs is a utopian vision—one that attempts to create "Heaven on earth," while blinded to the damage it causes within congregations. Theirs is an extreme radical outlook. The word *radical* itself has several definitions, some of them positive; as it is used throughout this work, it has a decidedly negative connotation. The extreme change advocated by those on the Left is not scriptural. On the contrary, it is dangerous.

It is hoped that this book will help brethren understand and deal with the problems posed by the New Left. It is my fervent prayer that

---

10. David Horowitz, *The Politics of Bad Faith* (Touchstone, 2000).

more and more congregations successfully overcome it. In this way the Lord's church can pursue the true mission given by Jesus: "Go ye into all the world, and preach the gospel to every creature" (Mark 16:15).

—David W. Hester

February 2007

CHAPTER TWO

Was Jesus a "Scholar"?

To ask the above question seems almost farcical. Our Lord, after all, is the Son of God. "Wherefore God also hath highly exalted him, and given him a name which is above every name" (Philippians 2:9). He is far superior to anything or anyone:

> Far above all principality, and power, and might, and dominion, and every name that is named, not only in this world, but also in that which is to come: and hath put all things under his feet, and gave him to be the head over all things to the church, which is his body, the fulness of him that filleth all in all (Ephesians 1:21–23).

As deity, He possesses all the characteristics of the other two members of the Godhead—including omnipotence.

However, it seems that some of the leaders of the New Left believe that Jesus is more in tune with academia than the "average" preacher, elder, deacon, or teacher. How often have those who are resistant to radical change in the church been denigrated as not having the spirit of Jesus? Indeed, Web sites abound which affirm that Jesus was Himself a "change agent"! Thus, those at the vanguard of the current movement attempt to co-op Jesus as being on their side; more sympathetic to academic seminars, papers, dissertations, and discussion groups than "out-of-date" gospel meetings in "backwater" congregations with preachers of no academic credentials.

What of it? Does Scripture give any support to such a view? To analyze this properly, one must look at the definition of the word *scholar*. Webster gives three meanings of the word: "One who attends a school of studies under a teacher; one who has done advanced study in a special field, a learned person; a holder of a scholarship."[1]

---

1. *Webster's Ninth New Collegiate Dictionary* (Springfield, Mass.: Merriam-Webster, 1991), 1051.

This three-pronged definition well fits the Sadducees, Pharisees, and lawyers of Jesus' day. The sect of the Sadducees was largely comprised of wealthy priests and Levites who believed only they had been given the right to interpret and apply the five books of Moses, which they believed were the only source of divine authority. The Pharisees, on the other hand, accepted all of the Old Testament as being inspired; applying to all aspects of life—but they also added oral tradition as the filter through which the Law had to be interpreted. "For the Pharisees, and all the Jews, except they wash their hands oft, eat not, holding the tradition of the elders" (Mark 7:3). The scribes were recognized as being the "official" scholars of the Books of Moses, so the Pharisees normally followed their lead—thus, the frequent usage of the phrase "scribes and Pharisees" in the Gospel accounts.

INTELLECTUAL ELITISM

When one examines the attitude of the "scholarly" classes of Jesus' time, he sees a striking similarity to some of the present day. John 7:14 states, "Now about the midst of the feast Jesus went up into the temple, and taught." The reaction of the Jews in verse 15 is quite enlightening: "And the Jews marvelled, saying, How knoweth this man letters, having never learned?"

If one cannot detect intellectual snobbery in this passage, it almost jumps off the page later in the chapter. After describing the division of opinion that existed among the people concerning Jesus, John writes: "Then came the officers to the chief priests and Pharisees; and they said unto them, Why have ye not brought him? The officers answered, Never man spake like this man" (John 7:45–46). Notice the response that was given: "Then answered them the Pharisees, Are ye also deceived? Have any of the rulers or of the Pharisees believed on him? But this people who knoweth not the law are cursed" (John 7:47–49).

To say that this passage shows the condescension of the "learned class" is an understatement. These individuals, who had been entrusted with the spiritual leadership of the people, felt nothing but contempt for them. Only those of their ilk would be accepted by them. The average man on the street, in their opinion, could not adequately interpret Scripture.

Is this far different from the "scholarly classes" of today? Now, to be sure, just because one has advanced degrees does not make him suspect. However, in religion in general, and in the Lord's church to some extent, there exists a number of men (and women) who have allowed themselves to be caught up in the elitist mentality just described. In some cases, the condescension and contempt for the average man in the pew is evident.

"HAVE YE NOT READ?"

What was Jesus' response to those of His day who were of the learned class? Over and again, Jesus called the Pharisees, Sadducees, and scribes back to the Scriptures. "Ye do err, not knowing the scriptures, nor the power of God" (Matthew 22:29). In the Sermon on the Mount, Jesus contrasted the tradition of the day with His teaching: "Ye have heard that it hath been said . . . but I say unto you . . ." In Matthew 12, He replied to the challenge of His enemies by twice saying, "Have ye not read." Jesus did not rely upon the learned class to interpret Scripture, but rather relied upon Scripture itself.

But how did Jesus regard Scripture? He clearly believed it to be inspired of God and authoritative. He attributed David's words in Psalms 110:1 to the Holy Spirit: "For David himself said by the Holy Ghost, The Lord said to my Lord, Sit thou on my right hand, till I make thine enemies thy footstool" (Mark 12:36). In Matthew 5:18, he said, "For verily I say unto you, Till heaven and earth pass, one jot or one tittle shall in no wise pass from the law, till all be fulfilled." How could He say this, if He did not believe all Scripture to be inspired and authoritative? His general attitude to Scripture is summarized in what He told the apostles in Luke 24:44. "And he said unto them, These are the words which I spake unto you, while I was yet with you, that all things must be fulfilled, which were written in the law of Moses, and in the prophets, and in the psalms, concerning me."

"THAT SAME JESUS"

When one considers Jesus, he must examine what Scripture says about Him. The Christ on this side of the cross is identical with the Christ of the personal ministry. "And many other signs truly did Jesus in the presence of his disciples, which are not written in this book:

but these are written, that ye might believe that Jesus is the Christ, the Son of God; and that believing ye might have life through his name" (John 20:30–31). Peter, in the sermon he delivered at Pentecost, spoke of "that same Jesus" (Acts 2:36). Indeed, "that same Jesus" is quite different from the picture often painted.

"That same Jesus" was in the beginning with God.

> In the beginning was the Word, and the Word was with God, and the Word was God. The same was in the beginning with God . . . And the Word was made flesh, and dwelt among us, (and we beheld his glory, the glory as of the only begotten of the Father,) full of grace and truth (John 1:1–14).

God made the world, and man, by Christ:

> Who is the image of the invisible God, the firstborn of every creature: for by him were all things created, that are in heaven, and that are in earth, visible and invisible, whether they be thrones, or dominions, or principalities, or powers: all things were created by him, and for him (Colossians 1:15–16).

When God said in Genesis 1:26, "Let us make man in our image, after our likeness," he was speaking to the preexistent Christ.

"That same Jesus" who was crucified, was raised from the dead. Peter declared this to be so in Acts 2:32: "This Jesus hath God raised up, whereof we all are witnesses." The disciples who saw Him could not have been deceivers, or deceived themselves.

> That which was from the beginning, which we have heard, which we have seen with our eyes, which we have looked upon, and our hands have handled, of the Word of life; (For the life was manifested, and we have seen it, and bear witness, and shew unto you that eternal life, which was with the Father, and was manifested unto us) (1 John 1:1–2).

Peter affirmed, "For we have not followed cunningly devised fables, when we made known unto you the power and coming of our Lord Jesus Christ, but were eyewitnesses of his majesty" (2 Peter 1:16). This same Jesus is now alive: "But now is Christ risen from the dead, and become the firstfruits of them that slept" (1 Corinthians 15:20).

"That same Jesus" is now Lord and Christ—our King. "Therefore let all the house of Israel know assuredly, that God hath made that same Jesus, whom ye have crucified, both Lord and Christ" (Acts 2:36). Contrary to what some of the Left affirm, the kingdom of God has come. Jesus declared, "Verily I say unto you, That there be some of them that stand here, which shall not taste of death, till they have seen the kingdom of God come with power" (Mark 9:1). In Acts 1:4, He told the apostles not to leave Jerusalem, "but wait for the promise of the Father." In verse 8 He said, "But ye shall receive power, after that the Holy Ghost is come upon you: and ye shall be witnesses unto me both in Jerusalem, and in all Judea, and in Samaria, and unto the uttermost part of the earth." This happened in Acts 2, when the apostles were baptized with the Holy Spirit and preached the first gospel sermon. As a result, about three thousand souls obeyed the truth; Acts 2:47 affirms, "And the Lord added to the church daily such as should be saved."

The Eternal Kingdom

The earthly manifestation of the kingdom is the church. Daniel 2:44 foretold its beginning.

> And in the days of these kings shall the God of heaven set up a kingdom, which shall never be destroyed: and the kingdom shall not be left to other people, but it shall break in pieces and consume all these kingdoms, and it shall stand for ever.

In chapter 7, Daniel even pinpoints when the kingdom would be established.

> I saw in the night visions, and, behold, one like the Son of man came with the clouds of heaven, and came to the Ancient of days, and they brought him near before him. And there was given him dominion, and glory, and a kingdom, that all people, nations, and languages, should serve him: his dominion is an everlasting dominion, which shall not pass away, and his kingdom that which shall not be destroyed (Daniel 7:13–14).

That this passage has reference to the ascension of Jesus to heaven there can be no doubt. After Jesus' return to heaven, the Father would give Him the kingdom.

One should note that there was a ten-day period between the ascension of Jesus to heaven and the preaching of the gospel at

Pentecost. This seems to be referring to the time of coronation, when the heavenly host would celebrate the triumphant return of Jesus, and would culminate in His being crowned king over His kingdom, the church.

HE IS COMING!

"That same Jesus" is now in heaven, preparing that wonderful place for us. Jesus declares in John 14:1–3,

> Let not your heart be troubled: ye believe in God, believe also in me. In my Father's house are many mansions: if it were not so, I would have told you. I go to prepare a place for you. And if I go and prepare a place for you, I will come again, and receive you unto myself; that where I am, there ye may be also.

He now serves as our great high priest. "Wherefore he is able also to save them to the uttermost that come unto God by him, seeing he ever liveth to make intercession for them" (Hebrews 7:25).

"This same Jesus, which is taken up from you into heaven, shall so come in like manner as ye have seen him go into heaven" (Acts 1:11). He will eventually come to judge the world. "For the Son of man shall come in the glory of his Father with his angels; and then he shall reward every man according to his works" (Matthew 16:27). "Behold, he cometh with clouds; and every eye shall see him, and they also which pierced him: and all kindreds of the earth shall wail because of him. Even so, Amen" (Revelation 1:7).

Those who hold to the premillennial view claim that Jesus will set up an earthly kingdom and reign on earth for a thousand years. As we have seen, the kingdom is already here—the church. Also, nowhere in the New Testament can be found any indication that Jesus will set one foot on this earth again—in fact, just the opposite is asserted.

> Marvel not at this: for the hour is coming, in the which all that are in the graves shall hear his voice, and shall come forth; they that have done good, unto the resurrection of life; and they that have done evil, unto the resurrection of damnation (John 5:28–29).

Paul wrote, "I charge thee therefore before God, and the Lord Jesus Christ, who shall judge the quick [living—dh] and the dead at his appearing and his kingdom" (2 Timothy 4:1). To assert otherwise is to contradict God's promise through Paul:

> Because he hath appointed a day, in the which he will judge the world in righteousness by that man whom he hath ordained; whereof he hath given assurance unto all men, in that he hath raised him from the dead (Acts 17:31).

He is the same loving Savior as ever; He is alive forevermore!

AUTHORITY: EXPLICIT AND IMPLICIT

In John 8:32 Jesus said, "Ye shall know the truth, and the truth shall make you free." If it is impossible for us to understand the word of God, then Jesus was a liar; of course, we know that such is not the case. Jesus' use of Scripture indicates that the Bible authorizes not only explicitly but also implicitly; and, we can infer what the Bible clearly implies. This is important, for there are some among us who seem to believe and teach that unless a thing is explicitly mentioned in the Bible, we cannot judge on matters not addressed. But think of the inherent contradiction in such a belief. Where is the explicit statement that only explicit statements in the Bible are applicable to mankind? Further, where in God's Word can anyone living today find his or her full name mentioned in connection with any command or statement? Obviously, the Bible authorizes with both explicit and implicit statements. When John writes, "For God so loved the world . . ." in John 3:16, all understand his or her name is implied in the verse. We can infer what the Bible clearly implies!

Jesus Himself reinforces the truth of this assertion in two passages of Scripture. The first is from Matthew 21:23–27:

> And when he was come into the temple, the chief priests and the elders of the people came unto him as he was teaching, and said, By what authority doest thou these things? and who gave thee this authority? And Jesus answered and said unto them, I also will ask you one thing, which if ye tell me, I in like wise will tell you by what authority I do these things. The baptism of John, whence was it? from heaven, or of men? And they reasoned with themselves, saying, If we shall say, From heaven; he will say unto us, Why did ye not then believe him? But if we shall say, Of men; we fear the people; for all hold John as a prophet. And they answered Jesus, and said, We

cannot tell. And he said unto them, Neither tell I you by what authority I do these things.

The Jews on this occasion saw all too well the obvious inference from the clear implication of Jesus' question to them.

The other passage is from Matthew 22:

> The same day came to him the Sadducees, which say that there is no resurrection, and asked him, saying, Master, Moses said, If a man die, having no children, his brother shall marry his wife, and raise up seed unto his brother. Now there were with us seven brethren: and the first, when he had married a wife, deceased, and, having no issue, left his wife unto his brother: likewise the second also, and the third, unto the seventh. And last of all the woman died also. Therefore in the resurrection whose wife shall she be of the seven? For they all had her (Matthew 22:23–28).

Quite obviously, they hoped to trap the Lord and "prove" their doctrine. However, they unwittingly had walked into a trap:

> Jesus answered and said unto them, Ye do err, not knowing the scriptures, nor the power of God. For in the resurrection they neither marry, nor are given in marriage, but are as the angels of God in heaven. But as touching the resurrection of the dead, have ye not read that which was spoken unto you by God, saying, I am the God of Abraham, and the God of Isaac, and the God of Jacob? God is not the God of the dead, but of the living (Matthew 22:29–32).

Notice that Jesus infers three things from Exodus 3:6; and further, He correctly infers what God clearly implies. First, Jesus infers that God was speaking to the Sadducees. Now, in the passage, God was directly addressing Moses; but the Lord held that Scripture is addressed to all people for all time. In this case, it applied to the Jews.

Second, the Son of God inferred that God was addressing the subject of the resurrection. In the passage from Exodus, God was telling Moses who He was and what to tell the Egyptians. The last thing on Moses' mind at that moment was the question of the resurrection! But from the statement by Jehovah, Jesus correctly inferred what God clearly implied.

This brings us to the third point. From God saying, "I am the God of Abraham, Isaac, and Jacob," Jesus inferred that God is not the God of the dead, but of the living. It is clear that Jesus believed inference may be utilized in areas where God clearly implies, and is authoritative because God implied it. Thus, we can use the same strategy today in areas where God clearly implies.

The Bible does not say, "Racism is wrong," but it implicitly teaches it is. Matthew 7:12 and James 2:1–9 clearly imply that racism is a sin against God and man. The parable of the Good Samaritan also implies the same important truth. It is evident that sound reasoning must be used in approaching any Bible subject, as Jesus Himself did.

Consider the impossibility of obeying God's Word if only explicit statements are applicable. If true, then the Bible would be a complicated document that would be impractical to carry from place to place, due to the tremendous size it would have! The Scriptures are a masterpiece of brevity and clarity, written so we can understand them. One does not have to obtain a college degree to arrive at a correct understanding; if that were true, then only a privileged few could properly interpret the Bible. That may well be what some of the leaders of the Left wish to happen. However, Jesus spoke where the common man could hear Him gladly. Such is still the case!

Jesus is the Master Teacher; He is the Great Physician. He is even called "Rabbi" on several occasions, by both friends and enemies— for they all acknowledged His ability to teach. However, the Lord still proclaims to His followers today,

> But be not ye called Rabbi: for one is your Master, even Christ; and all ye are brethren. And call no man your father upon the earth: for one is your Father, which is in heaven. Neither be ye called masters: for one is your Master, even Christ (Matthew 23:8–10).

No, Jesus was not a "scholar" in academia; He did not possess an advanced degree. He is, though, the King of kings and the Lord of lords—the Incarnate Word!

QUESTIONS FOR DISCUSSION

1. From the Gospel accounts, did Jesus have a close relationship with the "scholarly class"?

2. Did the Pharisees, scribes, and doctors of the law respect Jesus?

3. What was the most important tool Jesus used to answer the "scholars" of His day?

4. (True-False) Only explicit statements in Scripture are applicable to us today.

5. Can one find a passage of Scripture that explicitly states, "Racism is sinful"? If it is not explicitly stated, how can we determine whether or not it is true?

    Matt 7:12 ; James 2:1-9

How Shall We Interpret the Bible?

In 1994 I made the following statement in *Among the Scholars:*

> Strictly speaking, a liberal in religion is one who denies the inspiration of the Bible, the deity of Jesus, the virgin birth, and other basic Bible teachings. While it is quite possible, if not probable, that there are those among the scholars who are moving in that direction—if not already there—it would be a mistake to classify them in that category at present.[1]

While the latter part of that assertion may be true to a certain degree, the first part—dealing with the possibility of true liberals among the scholarly set—was even more correct than I realized at the time. Within a short period of time, articles and books appeared that tipped the hand of some as to their true beliefs. These writings have affected the way many interpret the Bible.

Indeed, as the above question poses, how shall we interpret the Bible? Is it just one of many "holy books"—no better or worse than, say, the Qu'ran of Islam, the Reg Veda of Hinduism, or the Book of Mormon? Is it nothing more than an outstanding piece of literature on par with the works of Shakespeare, "inspired" in the way that any great literary work is composed? Or is the Bible something much more—the very Word of God itself?

The way one responds to these questions will, to a large degree, determine his or her approach to Scripture. For if the Bible is nothing more than a human document, one does not have to follow it in any way. If the Bible is no better or worse than any other religious book, no one can know the mind of God. But if the Bible is God's Word, then we are obligated to lovingly do what our loving Father requires of us.

---

1. David W. Hester, *Among the Scholars* (Morris, AL: David W. Hester), 1994, 2.

INSPIRED OR EXPIRED?

With regard to the inspiration of Scripture, there are three views advocated. The liberal view affirms that the Bible contains the Word of God—that it is no more inspired than any piece of literature. This view holds that there are no miracles, and the supernatural can be explained away.

The neo-orthodox view affirms that the Bible becomes the Word of God. More will be said of this position later. While not going as far as the liberals, those who hold this view wish to sidestep the "problems" modern critical scholarship claim are inherent in the Bible.

The conservative view affirms that the Bible is the Word of God. It is the final revelation of God to man, and is inerrant. As 2 Timothy 3:16–17 states,

> All scripture is given by inspiration of God, and is profitable for doctrine, for reproof, for correction, for instruction in righteousness: that the man of God may be perfect, throughly furnished unto all good works.

Literally, the text states that all Scripture is "God-breathed"—a translation of one Greek word, *theopneustos*.

The controversy surrounding the inspiration of the Bible among churches of Christ in the late nineteenth century has been well documented by such historians as Earl I. West.[2] Likewise, the Christian Church's battle over the College of the Bible and subsequent division in 1968 is familiar to students of Restoration history in the works of Adron Doran, J. E. Choate, and William Woodson.[3]

Like those controversies of the past, today there are some of the scholarly set who are adopting a stance at variance with Scripture— in this case, one of neo-orthodoxy. Concerning the inspiration of the Scriptures, the neo-orthodox position is that the Bible becomes the Word of God by means of a personal encounter with God in an act of revelation. Basically, this stance claims there are errors in the Bible;

---

2. Earl Irvin West, *The Search for the Ancient Order Vol. 2* (Indianapolis: Religious Book Service, 1950), 221–91.

3. J. E. Choate and Adron Doran, *The Christian Scholar* (Nashville: Gospel Advocate, 1987), 103–21; J. E. Choate &William Woodson, *Sounding Brass and Clanging Cymbals* (Henderson: Freed-Hardeman University, 1990).

that a perfect God chose an imperfect channel—human words—to communicate with man; and that the Bible is not a book of propositional truth.[4]

"RETHINKING" INERRANCY AND INSPIRATION

Consider, for example, the case of Carroll D. Osburn, retired professor of Bible at Abilene Christian University. In 1996 he wrote *The Peaceable Kingdom*. In it he included an ominous-sounding chapter, "The Exegetical Matrix of the Quest for the Elusive Non-Sectarian Ideal." The chapter, like the book itself, takes a position on the inspiration of Scripture that, at best, is neo-orthodox; however, it more closely resembles classic theological liberalism.

Examine carefully what Osburn said of J. W. McGarvey's view of inspiration: "Nevertheless, he held that the autographs and the corrected Greek text of the NT are inerrant. Errors are detectable in the text, but they do not affect faith."[5] He went on to quote assertions made by some that the Gospels have certain contradictions in the text, and that they are not an objectively written piece of history.[6] Osburn is flirting with disaster.

Beginning in the mid-1990s, some within the New Left began to take positions that were just as bold as those Osburn advocated. One need only to carefully observe articles that have been written in scholarly journals to confirm this. We are told that we must undertake a "rethinking" of the concepts of inerrancy and inspiration. The claim is made that we are not being honest when we say the Scriptures are inerrant, for there must be (according to those advocating this) qualifications given. It is averred that many people have in mind a word-for-word dictation from God when considering the inerrancy of the Bible. In addition, it is argued that the dictation theory is widely held in churches of Christ. This, it is claimed, has adversely affected the way we have interpreted the Bible.

---

4. Norman L. Geisler & William E. Nix, *A General Introduction to the Bible* (Chicago: Moody, 1981), 40.
5. Carroll D. Osburn, *The Peaceable Kingdom* (Abilene, TX: Restoration Perspectives, 1993).
6. Ibid.

However, this conveniently overlooks the numerous articles and books that have been written by brethren over the years—material in which the mechanical dictation theory is denied and plenary verbal inspiration is confirmed. But while acknowledging the denial, those who advocate this say it makes no difference—the same theory (of dictation) is promoted. To buttress this point, quotations are given from scholars such as William Abraham, who claimed that writers such as B. B. Warfield "covertly" held to the dictation view. Notice, however, what D. A. Carson said in response to Abraham's claims:

> Certainly such writers occasionally use the word "dictation," but it has been shown repeatedly that many older writers use "dictation" language to refer to the *results* of inspiration, not its mode—i. e., the *result* was nothing less than the very words of God. As for the mode, Gaussen himself forcefully insists that the human authors of Scripture are not merely "the pens, hands, and secretaries of the Holy Ghost," for in much of Scripture we can easily discern "the individual character of the person who writes"[7] (emphasis in original—dh).

Yet, how do some brethren view the inspiration of the prophets, who often said, "Thus saith the Lord," and the other authors of the Bible? They claim that the inspiration of the various authors of the Bible cannot be equated with the Old Testament model of God speaking to the prophets and their declaring "Thus saith the Lord." It is claimed that such books as Psalms, Proverbs, the Gospels, historical narratives, and epistles don't come across with this same idea, which (it is claimed) implies that the authors were mere secretaries writing down the exact set of words God wanted recorded.

In addition, some attempt to make a distinction between the "word of God" and the Bible. Further, there are those who claim that in the message of the Bible we hear God speaking to our hearts. It is curious, indeed, what some on the Left seem to believe about what the Bible says about itself. Since the Bible does not use the word *inerrancy,* it is assumed that it has nothing to say about the subject. As for inspiration,

---

7. D. A. Carson, "Recent Developments In The Doctrine Of Scripture," in *Hermeneutics, Authority, and Canon* (Grand Rapids: Academie Books, 1986), 29–30.

since God's Word does not use theological terminology, it is assumed that what the Bible does say is vague. When Kings and Chronicles are compared to Romans and Galatians, it is assumed that the former are useless to the modern-day exegete.

"MOMENT OF MEANING"

It is concerning the process of inspiration, though, that one philosophy seems to come to the forefront. It is claimed that the Bible is not a dead letter to people today when it leads to the knowledge of God and spiritual life. This is plainly the neo-orthodox position on the inspiration of Scripture. One must have a "moment of meaning" for the Bible to become relevant in his life. As Archer observes, "According to this view, the Word of God is a dynamic principle which comes into operation only when there is a living or 'existential' encounter between the believer and God."[8] The Holy Spirit must act in some semi-direct way upon the heart of the reader. What shall we say to all of this?

The neo-orthodox view is subjectivism at its worst. If the Bible has errors in some places, then how can it be trusted in others? As Geisler and Nix say, "In no meaningful sense may God's authorship cover the whole of Scripture and, at the same time, the errors in Scripture."[9] Or, as Archer observes:

> Thus it turns out that every religious affirmation of the adherents of this school is ultimately dependent upon the truthfulness of the written Word of God, the Hebrew-Christian Scriptures. If these are erroneous in any portion, then they may be erroneous in any other portion; no reliance can be placed in them at all, or indeed in any affirmation which Neo-Orthodox theologians have derived from them—and all their doctrinal statements about God, encounter, and faith have in fact been derived from them.[10]

Concerning the means by which God communicated to the authors of the Bible, this view says that in the Bible a "word" is something

---

8. Gleason L. Archer, *A Survey of Old Testament Introduction, Revised and Expanded* (Chicago: Moody, 1994), 33.
9. Geisler & Nix, 41.
10. Archer, 35.

dynamic and alive. It is claimed that a word is more than simply speech; it is God acting. As stated before, the neo-orthodox position claims that God chose an imperfect channel of communication— human words. Archer makes some pertinent observations concerning this point:

> Thus, in their zeal to sidestep the assaults of rationalistic higher criticism upon the trustworthiness of the biblical record, and to rescue the significance of the Christian message in the face of scientific objections to the supernatural, the theologians of the Neo-Orthodox movement have resorted to a paradoxical view of the nature of revelation itself. They hold the position that by its very nature, divine revelation cannot be inscripturated. As soon as it is imprisoned in words, especially words setting forth propositions about God and spiritual truth, then it becomes the object of men's minds and cognitive powers. It thus falls under the control of man, and finds itself imprisoned within the covers of the written word. Revelation therefore is not to be equated with revealed doctrines or propositions about theology; rather, it consists of a direct encounter between God and man, as one subject confronting another subject.[11]

Further, this position proposes that God has "adjusted" His statements so that they are no longer perfectly true. However, McCartney and Clayton answer this by making three crucial points:

> First, Jesus Christ was here, and interacted with people face to face. If God can reveal Himself truly in the person of Jesus Christ, with all the limitations of being human, then He can certainly reveal Himself truly in language . . . when He was on earth He was truly and unequivocally God. The incarnation serves as the ultimate foundation for God's linguistic communication with us (Hebrews 1:1–3).
>
> Second, people can speak because God speaks. Language was not a human invention according to the Bible. God spoke first and by speaking created (Genesis 1) . . . He did assign to man the task of naming the animals and perhaps most things, but linguistically itself was given to man . . . Anything that can be said in one language and culture can be said in any other (although it may take longer in some languages than others) . . . Thus, although a particular language may influence the thought's form, it does not limit or determine thought.

---

11. Ibid., 33–34.

Third, according to the Bible, humans were made "in God's image." Therefore they have an innate ability to think thoughts patterned after God's thoughts. Linguistic communication from God to humans is possible, though never exhaustive, just as communication between people is possible though never exhaustive.[12]

GOD *CAN* COMMUNICATE WITH MAN

My wife, Brenda, is a speech-language pathologist with over twenty-five years of experience; consequently, I have access to her textbooks and notes concerning human communication—as well as her own insights into the subject. When a person sees the structure of the vocal cords and larynx and how they work in human speech, he immediately realizes God made us more than capable of communicating; and further, He surely can communicate with us! In fact, when I first broached this subject with my wife, her first reaction was to laugh and express her disbelief that some should take such an absurd position. Brenda's experience and insight into human communication has given her a deeper appreciation for the beauty of God's handiwork.

Jesus' usage of Scripture, as we have already seen, affirms that the Bible is inerrant. Over and again, He says, "It is written," and acknowledges the historicity of people, places, and events such as Noah (Luke 17:26–27), Jonah's fish experience (Matthew 12:40), the destruction of Sodom (Luke 17:29, 32), and Naaman's leprosy (Luke 4:27).

In addition, Jesus often based His arguments upon a single word or tense of a word. His defense of the resurrection in Matthew 22:32, as we have seen, is based upon the tense of the grammar of Exodus 3:6. Jesus answered the Pharisees in Matthew 22:45 by calling attention to one word—"Lord"—from Psalms 110:1. In John 10:34–35, which some brethren think is "tenuous" support for inerrancy, Jesus defended Himself by singling out one word from Psalms 82:6—"gods."

Finally, in Matthew 5:18, Jesus virtually affirmed His belief in verbal inspiration and inerrancy: "For verily I say unto you, till heaven and earth pass, one jot or one tittle shall in no wise pass from the law, till all be fulfilled." Paul's argument in Galatians 3:16 is based on one word from Genesis 17:7. "Now to Abraham and his seed were the

---

12. Dan McCartney & Charles Clayton, *Let The Reader Understand* (Wheaton: BridgePoint, 1994), 40–41.

promises made. He saith not, and to seeds, as of many; but as of one, and to thy seed, which is Christ."

INERRANCY IS SCRIPTURAL!

Contrary to the position under review, the Bible has a great deal to say about inspiration and inerrancy. Curiously, those who advocate this never touch 1 Corinthians 2:7–13. The passage reads as follows:

> But we speak the wisdom of God in a mystery, even the hidden wisdom, which God ordained before the world unto our glory: which none of the princes of this world knew: for had they known it, they would not have crucified the Lord of glory. But as it is written, Eye hath not seen, nor ear heard, neither have entered into the heart of man, the things which God hath prepared for them that love him. But God hath revealed them unto us by his Spirit: for the Spirit searcheth all things, yea, the deep things of God. For what man knoweth the things of a man, save the spirit of man which is in him? Even so the things of God knoweth no man, but the Spirit of God. Now we have received, not the spirit of the world, but the spirit which is of God; that we might know the things that are freely given to us of God. Which things also we speak, not in the words which man's wisdom teacheth, but which the Holy Ghost teacheth; comparing spiritual things with spiritual.

In verse 13 Paul sets forth how inspiration took place: "Which things also we speak, not in the words which man's wisdom teacheth, but which the Holy Ghost teacheth; comparing spiritual things with spiritual." Other translations more accurately render the phrase, "combining spiritual things with spiritual words." This ought to settle the issue once and for all concerning the nature of inspiration.

"A WITNESS TO GOD"—NOT *THE* WITNESS

Those who advocate neo-orthodoxy claim that the Bible is not the ultimate end. Instead, they say, it is a witness to God, Christ, and the Holy Spirit. It is then claimed that a witness is not identical with that to which it attests. Those who advance this view say that the Bible is revelatory as it points toward the will and nature of God. God is infallible and the word of God that we learn from the Bible will thus be infallible, it is claimed, but the two should not be confused.

Two things stand out when one carefully examines this position. First, notice that reference is made to the Bible as "a" witness to God, Christ, and the Holy Spirit. The indefinite article implies others are needed. How can one know anything about the Godhead without the Bible? What other witnesses does one have in mind? How could God not have also spoken through the Qu'ran, the Egyptian Book of the Dead, or from the Hindu Vedas, if this is true?

Second, an attempt is made—as we pointed out earlier—to separate "the word of God that we learn from the Bible." In other words, there are parts of the Bible that are not the word of God. This is simply one more example of the neo-orthodox position on inspiration in practice. It is merely an attempt to explain away difficult sections of the Bible.

It will not do to say on one hand the Bible is the final court of appeal in this world and that it reveals Jesus Christ to us, and on the other hand claim the Bible has inaccuracies and is not inerrant. It either is or it isn't. If it is wrong in one place, how are we to trust it in others?

In 2005 John Shelby Spong—a retired Episcopal bishop—published a book titled *The Sins of Scripture.* Being a liberal, Spong was eager to put forth his view of the Bible. He had earlier written *Rescuing the Bible from Fundamentalism,* which tipped his hand as to where he stood. Reading *The Sins of Scripture* seems like déjà vu, in light of what some brethren are saying.

Consider: "It is hard to maintain the claim of inerrancy in the face of biblical statements that are obviously incorrect. The 'Word of God' is not infrequently simply wrong."[13] How different is this from the position taken by Carroll Osburn? Of course, Spong goes further; he claims that all the miraculous events in the Bible never happened.[14] As far as we know, our brethren on the Left have not taken that position. But how long will it be before some do?

The Southern Baptist Convention faced an upheaval in the 1980s from "moderates" in their seminaries who affirmed that the Bible is

---

13. John Shelby Spong, *The Sins of Scripture* (San Francisco: HarperSanFrancisco, 2005), 19.
14. Ibid., 281–83.

not inerrant.[15] It is quite interesting, indeed, that some brethren quote extensively—with approval—from those who advocated that position during that time. Could it be that we in churches of Christ will fight the same battles our ancestors did in the late 1800s? We must be ready to withstand all attacks from the New Left and affirm what the Bible teaches about itself—that it is the inspired, inerrant Word of God.

QUESTIONS FOR DISCUSSION

1. Is it enough to say that the Bible is "inspired"?

2. Discuss the three views of the inspiration of Scripture. Which one is right?

3. Why is the neo-orthodox position dangerous?

---

15. Roy C. Honeycutt, "Biblical Authority: A Treasured Heritage!" RevExp 83/4 (1986), 605–22.

CHAPTER THREE

Among the Scholars—Again

The 1996 Christian Scholars Conference was held on the campus of David Lipscomb University July 18–20. As was the case in previous years, invitations were offered to various teachers, administrators, and preachers to submit papers. Having participated in the 1993 conference—which experience I detailed in *Among the Scholars*—I was issued an invitation to be a part of the conference.

The invitation presented me with a decision to make. I knew what to expect and the tenor of the event; most invited to participate were from the New Left with their own agenda. If the choice was made to participate, the impression could be given that I approved of the entire event. On the other hand, by this point many people were aware of my previous experience and subsequent reporting. On balance, choosing not to go would be passing up a golden opportunity.

After the decision was made to participate, the direction of my presentation became clear. Since many of the participants would know where I stood, I could not enjoy the luxury of "blending in" and remaining inconspicuous until the presentation, as had been the case at Harding. (Or, at least I had tried to be inconspicuous. The first night I was at Harding, I ate in the cafeteria along with the other participants. As I was getting my food, I dropped my tray. So much for being inconspicuous! To say I was embarrassed is an under-statement.) So my paper for presentation at Lipscomb—and the presentation itself—had to be direct and to the point.

"REFLECTIONS ON CURRENT PROBLEMS"

However, there would be no need of tipping my hand from the start. The title I chose for the presentation was innocuous, at least at first blush: "Reflections on Current Problems among Churches of Christ: A Proposal." I began the paper with three real-life situations, all related to the current state of affairs with the New Left. The first—a conversation between a preacher and his physician transpired between my dad, Benny Hester, and his doctor the year before.

The physician had kept my dad apprised of the trouble that had occurred at his home congregation; these problems had arisen because of a group within the church that had become denominational. The preacher of the congregation later told me that the group became very childish. They all sat in one section of the auditorium. When one from their group did not lead singing, they slammed their songbooks shut— whipping them into their laps, and crossing their arms, refusing to sing!

When the group finally left the congregation, they moved to a small, rural church and tried to take it over. The elders at that congregation took steps to prevent it from happening, and they finally left there as well. During that time, a relative of one of the members of the divisive group wrote a letter to the elders of that rural church, lambasting the leadership for daring to stand against the winds of change. This man who wrote the letter was preaching in a large city at the time, and his father-in-law was a ringleader of the divisive group. The preacher's father-in-law had also attended Woodmont Hills in Nashville. The preacher's father-in-law has since left the church, and at last report was trying to divide the denomination where he was attending!

TRACK RECORD OF TURMOIL

The second real-life situation described the division that took place at the Chisholm Hills Church of Christ in Florence, Alabama, in 1993. The preacher, Joe VanDyke, refused to preach against the use of instrumental music in worship, among other things, and was subsequently relieved of his duties by the elders. The elders scheduled a congregational meeting to explain their reasons. The meeting quickly degenerated into a squabble, according to one of the members present that day. As a result, half of the congregation left, taking with them half of the contribution. The Magnolia Church of Christ was thus formed, and in short order began open fellowship with denominations.

Something that I found intriguing was that those involved in the Chisholm Hills division were themselves no strangers to congregational turmoil. In fact, the core leaders of the group had been involved in several church splits in the Shoals area over the past fifteen years.

An oft-repeated claim made after the fact was that "no one talked to Joe," or "I wish someone had tried to study with him," as if no one had taken the time to try to steer VanDyke away from the course he was pursuing. The truth is simpler. The Chisholm Hills elders made efforts for at least a year prior to the division to keep VanDyke from drifting away. One of the elders, in fact, had been a close friend of VanDyke for many years, and was deeply hurt by VanDyke's apostasy. His grief was something I attempted to capture as I described the incident.

A COURAGEOUS STAND

The third vignette I included was more hopeful. It described an older gospel preacher—Fred Dillon—busily typing a monthly progress report of his work with the elderly and infirm in the Shoals area. Only this time his report took on a sense of urgency. He had also been greatly troubled by the events that led to the formation of the Magnolia congregation, and its subsequent open fellowship with the denominations. He also was disturbed by reports from other congregations, some who were supporting him financially in his work.

Fred Dillon is a well-known preacher in Florence, Alabama. In fact, he is what could be called a "Renaissance man," having served as the editor of the local newspaper for many years, and then as the campus minister at the University of North Alabama. Fred is a sound preacher who loves the Lord and loves souls. His letter to supporting congregations on this occasion reflected that love. He declared his refusal of financial support from any congregation that supported the leftist agenda. His courageous stand drew the hearty support of the vast majority of brethren in the Florence area.

EXTREME RADICALISM—AN ONGOING PROBLEM

After including the events just described, my paper addressed an underlying reason for the change movement. The concept of change is not wrong, in and of itself; rather, it is change not in keeping with the Word of God that is the problem. An underlying reason for the push for radical change in churches of Christ is much the same as what took place during the "anti" movement which began in the 1940s. In essence, I summarized one of the theses of *Among the Scholars* in making this point. Extreme radicalism has been a thorn in the side of the Lord's church, on both the Right and the Left. It affects how the world views us, as well as our effectiveness in spreading the gospel.

I then proceeded to address two fundamental questions facing congregations. The first dealt with the purpose of baptism. It was shown that the New Testament clearly indicates that salvation is the purpose of baptism. Reasons from Scripture were given and emphasized.

The second question addressed the matter of open fellowship. In making the case against such, I focused on 2 John 9–11, a key passage. I affirmed that the "doctrine of Christ" refers to the doctrine Jesus and His apostles taught. Other passages of Scripture were cited to support my position.

As I drew the paper to its conclusion, I made the "proposal" referred to in the title. It was a call for those leading the change movement to cease and desist. Jesus' prayer to the Father in Gethsemane, as well as His earlier prayer for unity, were cited. The assumption was made that those on the Left are responsible for the divisions among us; I believed it then; I still believe it today.

THE 1996 SEMINAR—A KALEIDOSCOPE OF DOCTRINES

Thus, after submitting the paper, I made ready for the seminar. As the weekend drew near, I was invited to participate in a lectureship in Kentucky, following my presentation in Nashville. I gladly accepted, welcoming the friendly venue to offset the hostile reaction I expected to receive at Lipscomb. There was a bit of uncertainty present, as had been the case in 1993; however, in this case it was concerning the amount of hostility I would face. Would it affect the presentation itself?

One welcome difference from 1993 was that I was not alone. There would be some friendly faces in the audience. My dad decided to make the trip to Lipscomb, along with a preacher friend of his from Walker County, Alabama. They would meet me on campus, on the day of my presentation.

As I settled in, I took in my surroundings. Those attending the conference had a unique look, to say the least. You know the type— skinny, academic types with bushy mustaches and goatees, backpacks at the ready. It was indeed amusing to observe them interact with each other, and to seriously consider inane concepts.

I had already decided, in the days leading up to the conference, not to attend as many of the sessions as I had in 1993. One reason was purely practical: I needed to reserve energy for my presentation in Kentucky. But the other reason was more to the point. I had determined that this would be the last Christian Scholars Conference I would attend, so I wanted my presentation to be as focused and as forceful as I could make it. This could happen only if I had time to myself.

While none of the sessions were as outrageous as those of the 1993 event, they nonetheless were strange, to say the least. For example, there was a presentation concerning effective ways to incorporate drama into church assemblies—complete with a video presentation! No matter that God's Word does not indicate any support for such in worship.

Then there was the session that addressed Foy E. Wallace's debates with Charles Neal on premillennialism. The gentleman making the presentation—Douglas A. Foster—is infamous for his twisting of the truth concerning Restoration preachers and their writings, as we shall point out in a later chapter. Foster was unquestionably biased against Wallace and in favor of Neal, and that bias colored his presentation. The troubling thought was that those not familiar with the true history—as told in Earl I. West's *Search for the Ancient Order,* and in the debate book published by Wallace himself—would take Foster's version of history and analysis as what actually happened.

HARDEMAN'S SERMONS SCORNED

However, it was Carl McKelvey's presentation, just before mine, that was most irksome. Being one of the vice-presidents of Lipscomb, McKelvey was in a unique position. As it was, he chose a puzzling course. His focus was on the *Hardeman Tabernacle Sermons,* delivered in the Ryman Auditorium in Nashville. Specifically, McKelvey contended that published attendance figures—by both the *Nashville Banner* and subsequent brotherhood books, such as Earl West's *Search* and articles—were full of lies. According to published reports at the time, when the first meeting was held in March-April of 1922, the

Ryman was "packed and jammed," with 6000–8000 people, with an estimated 2000–3000 being turned away.

But McKelvey would have none of it. In taking issue with the attendance figures, he was conveniently rebutting the testimony of people who had already passed away, as well as respected Restoration historians like Earl West. One had to wonder, what purpose did this serve? Why attempt to tear down a great event that had such a positive impact for the cause of Christ, and is still affecting people for good today?

Throughout the day, I had been sitting by my dad, who was squirming in his seat—wishing he could give a rebuttal to Foster, and now to McKelvey. Unfortunately, Foster's lecture was designed for little or no feedback; McKelvey used all his time, leaving none for questions. Needless to say, Dad and his friend were spoiling for a chance to respond.

A POSITIVE REACTION

For the presentation, I determined to diverge a bit from the printed text, adding material to further explain where I was coming from, doctrinally speaking. At first, I did not know if I would have enough time; but, the young fellow who immediately preceded me graciously gave me the remainder of his time.

I decided to list my stand on various doctrinal questions from the New Testament, in order that there be no doubt. I inserted this material just before I addressed the two questions mentioned earlier. Since I had extra time, I was under no time constraints.

Two huge differences between the 1993 conference and this one was the size of the audience and the feedback I received after I finished. In '93 the venue was a regular-sized classroom, three-quarters filled. In '96, the venue was a large lecture hall—completely filled. Also, in attendance in '96 were some interesting characters. One was John Mark Hicks, who at the time was a professor at Harding Graduate School, and a Rubel Shelly apologist. Another in attendance was an elder at Magnolia Church of Christ. I had engaged in a lengthy written correspondence with this elder about various doctrinal questions about which he and I differed. We had also discussed fellowship issues that

Magnolia obviously had with the brethren in the greater Florence area. Now I saw him for the first time.

The reaction to my presentation was quite different from '93. At Harding, there had been no audible response—although for everyone else, there was at least polite applause. This time, though, it was different. After a half-second pause, dad's friend started clapping loudly with his big bear-paw hands, thus starting a chain reaction. This was possibly the only time many of these people would positively react to the truth!

A Calm and Polite Discussion—To a Point

I used the extra time for questions. At Harding only two questions were asked, but on this occasion at Lipscomb I fielded many more. Although significant differences of opinion were evident, the tenor of the discussion that ensued was calm.

One young man attempted, in the framework of his question, to shift the blame of division from those on the Left to those "on your side of the fence." He referred to incidents of congregations dividing because of the bad attitudes displayed by those wanting to resist change. In responding, I conceded that in some cases there have been those who have displayed an un-Christian spirit, thus contributing to internal discord. However, I did not back down from my thesis: In the current movement to "change" the church, those on the Left bear the lion's share of the blame for whatever divisions ensue.

Others who asked questions wanted clarification on statements I had made during the presentation; again, all done in a calm manner. I knew there were those in the audience who attended congregations in Nashville that were at the forefront of the change movement; in fact, an elder from Otter Creek was present. Even he was polite, though.

As the discussion unfolded, one gentleman complimented me for coming and presenting what I believed in a civil manner. He praised the civility of the discussion, and lamented that not all discussions within our congregations had that tone. I thanked him, and fielded the next question, which had to do with proselytizing. In my "proposal," I suggested that those on the Left cease their attempts to sway unsuspecting brethren to their position, and thus divide the church.

In clarifying the issue, I referred to a leader of the Left who decries the "lack of autonomy in our churches." He says we violate it all the time. Then he goes across the country and does the very thing he decries by spreading his doctrine in both sermons and books. In so doing, he clearly violates church autonomy. Though I did not mention his name, the person to whom I was referring was Rubel Shelly.

John Mark Hicks, while silent to this point, remained silent no longer. After some in the audience objected, saying, "But he's invited to come," Hicks threw up his hand to be acknowledged. When he spoke, he attempted to respond by defending Shelly, not mentioning his name. Clearly Hicks knew exactly who I was referring to. When I stuck to my point, Hicks tartly retorted, "That doesn't seem very civil to me."

By this time, my dad had had enough. He raised his hand to be acknowledged, and I could tell he was ready to vent his frustration. However, my dad is also a master of self-control in moments of controversy, stemming from years of experience as a gospel preacher. He began in a carefully controlled voice.

> I have been listening to several people make their presentations today, and I have heard things that I know not to be the case. I have heard, for example, that Foy E. Wallace Jr. was to blame for the division over premillennialism in the 1930s. That is not so. I have heard just a little while ago that we lied when we said a great number of people came to hear N. B. Hardeman. That is not so. And now, it is alleged that we are not civil when we are pointing out the inconsistency of some who are actively dividing the church. That simply is not so. I think we'd better examine ourselves before we begin to make such outrageous claims.

I was outwardly appearing calm, with no visible sign of emotion; inwardly, I was yelling, "Go, Dad! That's the way!"

The bell had rung, so Hicks, McKelvey, and others made their way to the door to leave. Others began to file out, as well. I took a couple of further questions, and then ended the session. Several individuals came and shook my hand out of grudging respect. Others, I could tell, truly appreciated my willingness to expound on what I believed.

"KEEP ON PREACHING THE TRUTH"

Two of the men who came to me were interesting. One was a faculty member at Lipscomb—the man who complimented the civility of the discussion. As he drew close, he looked one way, then the other, and whispered in my ear, "Keep on preaching the truth, brother." Although I thanked him, I was startled by the way he said it. Was he so afraid of his job that he had to make sure President Hazelip wasn't looking when he complimented someone like me?

The other man was a faculty member at Abilene Christian University, of all places. I had never met him; I knew him because a couple of books he had written. He was not a member of the Bible faculty, and he assured me that there were far more people than I realized who did not agree with the direction in which ACU had been headed—although he did agree with me that too much damage had already been done. He complimented the lesson I had presented, and encouraged me to keep on preaching the truth. When I asked him about a recent speech made by Bill Banowsky at the ACU Lectureship, in which Banowsky called in effect for open fellowship, the gentleman replied, "I wouldn't walk across the campus to hear Bill Banowsky speak." This heartened me. While it was too late to bring the Bible faculty back to the truth, at least there were still some fighting from the inside to affect positive change of their own—the kind that adheres to God's Word.

I eventually made my way over to my dad and his friend, who wished me well. Daddy hugged me and complimented the job I did, which meant more than anything I had heard. After we said goodbye, I set off for Kentucky—and a much friendlier welcome than I had received in Nashville.

Since then, I have thought often about that weekend. Did it do any good? I hope so. The things I said that day were from the heart, from the Scriptures, and intended to change attitudes. Only time and eternity will tell how much of an impact my efforts made. Although I have resolved never to return to the Christian Scholars Conference— I've said all that I needed to say—I encourage everyone to take whatever opportunity is afforded them to speak the truth to those who need to hear it. God's Word, so presented, can make a positive impact in the lives of erring brethren.

QUESTIONS FOR DISCUSSION

1. How do you feel about the Christian Scholars Conference?

2. Is it troublesome that several schools participate in this event? Why?

3. Do we need to take every opportunity afforded us to present the truth? Why?

CHAPTER FOUR

Reflections on Current Problems among Churches of Christ: A Proposal

"They Know Better"

The doctor closed the door behind him and turned toward the patient with a concerned look on his face. He had finished the yearly examination; nothing was amiss. Rather, the concern he exemplified was on a higher plane—that which is spiritual. The physician was also an elder at the local congregation; had been for many years. The patient was a preacher for a congregation in another county. They often discussed their common fears, dreams, and insights.

"I've seen things happen in the congregation over the past year that I thought I'd never see," the doctor said. He went on to explain how the congregation had experienced a split when a contingent insisted on having its way above the wishes of the elders. This situation had been brewing for several months; the elders had exhausted every avenue in trying to reason with them. Even now, as he talked, tears welled up in the eyes of the doctor.

"They could not stand the preaching they were hearing from the pulpit," he said. The preacher for the church, who was well known for not only his knowledge of Scripture but also his balance, had preached a sermon concerning the "change" movement, in which he outlined several areas that were not biblical. The contingent demanded the preacher be reprimanded. When the elders made it clear they stood behind the preacher, the trouble began.

"We've known these people for a long time. We watched some of them grow up. They know better. If they would come back to us, we would throw our arms around them and gladly take them back. As it stands now, there is division."

A Time for Tears

The atmosphere in the auditorium was one of chaos. The preacher for the large city congregation had just "come out of the closet," as it were, with his doctrinal views that were at odds with the elders and about half the congregation. As a result, the elders had called a meeting of the church for this day, to make known the reasons for his dismissal. It quickly degenerated, as those opposed to the elders began venting long-held animosities and declaring where they were: opposed to anything the elders said and behind everything the preacher proclaimed.

After the meeting concluded and the opposition had left, a deacon spotted one of the elders standing off to one side with his head bowed. When he approached him, the deacon noticed the tears flowing down the elder's face. This was a man who had been dedicated to missions and teaching young men; he was not a man who could be called a radical, by any means. He had been a close friend with the preacher; now, that friendship was broken.

The deacon put his arm around him. "Don't worry, brother. I'm going to stand with you and the elders through this, and there's a lot more who will do the same thing." The elder raised his head, and through the tears, asked, "Why? Why do they insist on dividing the church of my Lord?"

"Stop Dividing The Church"

As he typed his report, the preacher stopped and pondered the significance of what he was doing. He had been preaching the gospel about a half-century. Now he was ministering to the elderly and infirmed. Although he was supported by several congregations—had been for many years—word had reached him that a couple of those churches were beginning to advocate practices and doctrines not in keeping with the Bible. After investigating for himself, he had confirmed that conclusion. So he was going to send a letter to the elders of all his supporting churches (privately) asking them not to support him further if they held to said practices and doctrines.

He realized the two churches in question might very well do just that; however, he was ready to bear the hardship involved in lost support. His conviction concerning truth outweighed the fear of what would happen. As he resumed typing, his convictions were expressed on paper firmly, yet from the spirit which characterized the man—humility and love for souls. He had toiled in Midwestern states where the church was barely known; he himself had come out of denominationalism, and thought that many were clamoring to go back to what he had left so many years before.

The climax of his letter summed up his thoughts concerning those teaching different doctrines and attempting to influence others. "Why don't they stop dividing brethren and get about the business of preaching the gospel?"

DIVISION: WHO IS TO BLAME?

Indeed, there are many brethren asking that very question. The three incidents described above are based on actual events. They are symptomatic of what is occurring in churches of Christ across this country. At this good hour, brethren are being threatened with—if not already experiencing—outright division. Under the banner of "change" and "renewal," some are demanding their way—or no way.

Now, please do not misunderstand. The concepts of change and renewal are right and good, when understood in a biblical context. The sinner must change his ways; the lethargic brother or sister must change his/her attitude and actions; the lukewarm or dead church must change in keeping with the Lord's will. No, it is not the concepts of change and renewal that are troubling. It is what is being done to congregations that once were at peace that is disturbing.

In far too many cases, there are brethren insisting that the church change fundamental beliefs about basic Bible teaching. While ostensibly done for a noble purpose, the end result always seems to be the same. I know personally of five congregations in north Alabama over the past four years that have been rent asunder over specific doctrinal issues. Brethren once united in purpose and precept are now split, almost irrevocably. Congregations that once worked closely together are now separated from one another because of the teaching being done by some.

In many ways the situation is eerily reminiscent of the major controversy that engulfed churches of Christ beginning in the 1940s: the orphans' home/cooperation question. During that time, a contingency of brethren demanded their way or no way in forcing congregations to accept the position against orphans' homes and cooperation. In fact, the contentions were so sharp that division ensued. The effects of that controversy are still being felt.

Because of the extremism of some in the "anti" movement, an entire generation was negatively affected. The harsh attitudes exhibited by some, along with unethical tactics by a few, pushed many from the extreme right to the extreme left. As a result, churches of Christ are experiencing problems which threaten it with another major rupture along the lines of the 1906 division.

BIBLICAL ANSWERS

It shall be our task in this book to examine the major questions facing congregations today, see what God's Word says, and give biblical answers. Then we will suggest a proposal to consider when dealing with these matters.

Before we begin, though, it would be good to look at what God told Joshua:

> Only be thou strong and very courageous, that thou mayest observe to do according to all the law, which Moses my servant commanded thee: turn not from it to the right hand or to the left, that thou mayest prosper whithersoever thou goest (Joshua 1:7).

Notice that God told Joshua not to turn to the right or the left. This principle can be found in the New Testament. In Romans 14 Paul admonishes us not to bind matters of opinion on brethren (corresponding to the "right hand"). In 2 John 9–11 and 1 Corinthians 4:6 we are told not to "go beyond" or "transgress" what is written (corresponding to "the left"). The New Testament stresses balance throughout.

Baptism

The first question we must address is, what is the purpose of baptism? Must one understand the purpose of baptism before he submits to it? There are many brethren attempting to persuade people that we must not be dogmatic about the purpose of baptism; that we may accept denominational baptism, even though it may not be for the purpose of being saved.

It is our contention, however, that the design of baptism is to save (Mark 16:16). Baptism is a condition for remission of sins and it never stands alone. It is always associated with faith and repentance. Apart from these it has no value. The power lies in the blood of Christ, which is contacted in baptism.

In saying that baptism saves, we are still saying that we are saved by faith; that we are saved by grace; that we are saved by the blood; and that we are saved by God's righteousness and not man's (Hebrews 11:6; Ephesians 2:8–9; 1:7; Romans 10:1–3). The fact remains, though, that baptism is a part of the Great Commission.

Baptism cannot undervalue the atonement, for it is resting upon and deriving its value from the name of Christ. Baptism cannot disparage the work of the Spirit, since by the gospel the Spirit calls men to believe and repent. It is by one Spirit that we are all baptized into the one body (1 Corinthians 12:13). Baptism does not contradict God's grace, because baptism belongs to the grace of God. Baptism does not nullify passages on salvation by faith, since it is an act of faith.

It is quite evident from the specific cases of conversion in the book of Acts that those converted understood clearly why they were being immersed. In fact, when one reads the account of the conversion of the Ethiopian eunuch, Luke is exact in his detail. Acts 8 says that when Philip taught the eunuch, he "began at the same scripture, and preached unto him Jesus" (Acts 8:35). The next verse says, "And as they went on their way, they came unto a certain water: and the eunuch said, See, here is water; what doth hinder me to be baptized?" Verses 38 and 39 provide a record of Philip's baptizing him.

The point? To preach Christ is to preach the necessity of being baptized! Peter plainly told those on Pentecost to be baptized "for the remission of sins" (Acts 2:38). Paul himself was told to be baptized to "wash away thy sins" (Acts 22:16). Can anyone deny that believing, penitent ones must understand the purpose of baptism—to be saved?

Open Fellowship with Denominationalism

A second question that must be considered is this: May we have open fellowship with those in the denominations, or those practicing doctrinal error? Again, there are those attempting to force the issue upon congregations that are not willing to lay down their opposition to such practices.

In 2 John 9–11, the apostle warned:

> Whosoever transgresseth, and abideth not in the doctrine of Christ, hath not God. He that abideth in the doctrine of Christ, he hath both the Father and the Son. If there come any unto you, and bring not this doctrine, receive him not into your house, neither bid him God speed: for he that biddeth him God speed is partaker of his evil deeds.

It is our contention this passage refers to what Jesus and His apostles taught. This would include the question about Jesus, as well as His teaching in every area of Christianity. The book *Among the Scholars* details our position concerning the passage. Suffice it to say, the preponderance of evidence, we believe, supports this position.

Given that conclusion, the passage would forbid the child of God to have fellowship with those who teach and practice doctrinal error. That is what Paul warned the Christians about in such passages as 1 Corinthians 4:6 and Galatians 1:6–11. Indeed, the warning John records in Revelation 22:18–19, while applying immediately to Revelation, applies as well to the entirety of the New Testament.

Jesus Himself warned: "But in vain they do worship me, teaching for doctrines the commandments of men" (Matthew 15:9). He also said: "And why call ye me, Lord, Lord, and do not the things which I say?" (Luke 6:46). Given His warnings against false teachers and admonitions to do what He says in Matthew 7:15–17, it would seem the Lord is quite concerned with our following His way and not man's.

This is not to say those in denominationalism are not sincere, or that we are to have nothing to do with them. It is simply saying this: we cannot embrace the teachings and practices of men that contradict plain Bible teaching. We must not go back into spiritual Egypt.

Cease and Desist!

This brings us to our proposal. In light of the current situation among churches of Christ, as exemplified by the cases alluded to at the beginning, the proposal seems to be obvious. If put into practice, much trouble would be avoided. It is simply this: May those leading the charge against "mainline" churches of Christ desist from exporting their teaching to other congregations and quit trying to proselytize brethren.

Again, this is spoken from years of observation. In the divisions alluded to at the beginning, attempts were made—and are still being made—to sway unsuspecting brethren to their position, so more divisions have ensued. Given what the New Testament says about those who cause division (Romans 16:17–18), it would seem that those involved in the recruitment would be given pause. Alas, though, such does not happen.

In the very shadow of the cross, with His pores oozing blood and in a state of physical shock, Jesus Christ prayed to the Father. He knew what was going to happen to Him; however, He also knew that God's plan had to be fulfilled. So with the disciples slumbering and His enemies near, the Lord prayed: "Father, if thou be willing, remove this cup from me: nevertheless not my will, but thine, be done" (Luke 22:42). Sadly, many today say: "Not Thy will, but mine be done." They do this to the point of splitting churches.

The Lord had earlier prayed in the presence of the eleven for the unity of His followers (John 17:20–21). Is it not strange that some who call for unity bring division?

By now the curious reader may be wondering: whom does this writer represent? In the immediate sense, I represent only myself. But in a very real sense, I represent hundreds—nay, thousands—of brethren who are concerned about the future of the church.

- I represent the elders who stay up until all hours of the night grappling for a way to stem false teaching and still hold the congregation together, all the while shedding tears over beloved brethren who are swept away.

- I represent the obscure preacher, toiling in his local work, preaching sound, practical lessons and attempting to make a difference in individual lives. He will never lay down his opposition to the radical change facing him.

- I represent those who have come out of denominationalism to embrace New Testament Christianity, only to be dismayed to see some clamoring to go back into what they had come out of years before.

- I represent the congregations ranging from thirty to three hundred to a thousand, who are bound and determined to stay with the truth of God's Word and resist any attempt to alter it.

In short, I represent those who are fully aware of what is happening in churches of Christ and will never, never, never give in. As for me, until the last breath of life expires from this mortal body, I have determined to meet and answer those who would split the body of my Lord. It is my fervent prayer that all of us will do the same.

Questions for Discussion

1. What was your first reaction to the three incidents mentioned at the beginning of the chapter?

2. Is all change necessarily wrong? Support your answer.

3. Why must the purpose of baptism be understood?

4. May we have fellowship with anyone we please? Why?

CHAPTER FIVE

"Instrumental Music Is Not a Salvation Issue"—But We Will Have It, Regardless!

The December 12, 2006 issue of *The Christian Chronicle* had a front-page article that was interesting. It read in part:

> The Richland Hills church in Texas—the largest of the nation's 13,000 a cappella Churches of Christ—has decided to add an instrumental worship assembly with communion on Saturday nights. Jon Jones, an elder and former pulpit minister at the 6400-member church, told the congregation December 3 that Richland Hills' elders "fully and completely" endorsed the decision. "There is unity in our eldership, and we are so thankful for that," Jones told church members at a combined adult Bible study, according to a video on the church Web site. Elder Roger Dean characterized the congregation's overall response as "extremely positive." "Frankly, we did not know what to expect," Dean said. "We felt like it was going to be pretty difficult, but it has not been . . . People are truly supporting the leadership and the eldership."[1]

On the Richland Hills website, there is this statement by the elders:

> With unity of spirit, the leadership of the Richland Hills Church of Christ has decided to add a third weekend assembly in 2007 that will include instrumental praise as part of this vision and mission. Former elders who participated in the three-year period of studies, fasting, and prayer for God's vision continue to be active members of the church body and are in support of the elders.[2]

---

1. Bobby Ross Jr., "Nation's largest Church of Christ adding instrumental service," *Christian Chronicle* (December 12, 2006) http://www. christianchronicle.org/modules.php?name=News&file=article&sid=555.
2. http://www.rhchurch.org/praise/Both-And_Church.html.

Rick Atchley—the preacher at Richland Hills—also preached a series of three sermons that are included on the website. They constitute the boldest defense of the use of instrumental music made by a preacher of churches of Christ in a hundred years.

The September 19, 2003 issue of *The Christian Chronicle* featured a similarly provocative article:

> What does it mean that five urban churches affiliated with churches of Christ have added instrumental worship services since the spring of 2001? Do such actions, which violate a long-held and deeply-revered doctrinal tenet of churches of Christ, represent the beginning of an avalanche?
>
> Or are the actions of five churches inconsequential in a fellowship of 13,200 congregations?
>
> Could such reflect even more important shifts in attitudes within churches of Christ toward Scripture and doctrine?
>
> The discussion was brought to the fore in late August by the decision, reported September 6 in the *San Antonio Express-News,* that the Oak Hills church, the nation's second-largest congregation led by prominent author and minister Max Lucado, will add an instrumental service in coming months.
>
> Other churches known to have added instrumental services— besides 3,800-member Oak Hills—include Northwest, Seattle, the largest in that region; Amarillo South, Texas; Farmer's Branch, Texas; and Southlake Boulevard, in the Dallas/Forth Worth area.[3]

Nearly one hundred years after the division with the Christian Church, churches of Christ are now seeing the same issues come to the forefront again. And in so doing, the same result takes place. Although, to read the report in the *Chronicle,* one would think that instrumental music is just what the church needs.

> The churches who have added instrumental services cite a common motivation—evangelism and outreach. All report increases in attendance since the switch.
>
> • The Southlake Boulevard church added a Sunday morning instrumental service in March, in addition to an a cappella

---

3. Lindy Adams, "Instrumental worship: isolated or key trend?" *Christian Chronicle* 60/10 (Oct. 2003), http://sites.silaspartners.com/partner/ Article_Display_Page/0,,PTID25485 | CHID127205 | CIID1639872,00.html.

service. Minister Keith Luttrell says, "Relevance is driving it. Relevance to our community. Reaching out to seekers." Luttrell said attendance overall has grown from 650 to 850 people, with more than 600 attending the instrumental service.

- Northwest, Seattle, added a Sunday night instrumental service in spring 2001, in addition to a morning a cappella service, says Bill Lawrence, pastoral minister. Lawrence said the service was added to reach the unchurched. After dropping from 500 to 470 people, attendance has grown to 550.

- Farmers Branch added a 6:00 P.M. Saturday instrumental service in September 2002, in addition to two Sunday morning a cappella services, says minister Chris Seidman. Preaching and children's classes are offered all three times. Attendance has grown from 1,000 people to 1,400, with 375 attending on Saturday. The new participants, he says, are "people with religious backgrounds, but who haven't gone for some time. They were worn out with the same old thing."

- The Body of Christ at Amarillo South, changed to all-instrumental services in February 2002. The congregation dropped from 900 to 700 people, but the attendance has grown to 1200, says minister Brad Small. The congregation considers itself a non-denominational community church.[4]

AN ERRONEOUS CONCLUSION

What is particularly interesting is the rationale for introducing instruments into worship. When one examines the document produced by the Farmers Branch congregation, for example, he reads these curious statements:

> The purpose of this presentation is to set forth what the leadership believes the Lord's will to be for the Farmers Branch Church concerning vocal and instrumental musical expression. The intent of this effort is not to test one's relationship with the Lord, or to define a belief system required for membership in this church, or to despise or judge anyone who does not agree with this position. Acceptance is not conditioned on any particular view of music. The intent is to articulate the leadership's view so that members, and especially prospective members, may know the church's position on this matter. This flexibility results from the *belief that music, vocal*

---

4. Ibid.

and / or instrumental, is not a "salvation issue," and thus is not one of the core beliefs of this church.

. . . The leadership believes that music lifted up in praise to God and His Son is an outpouring from the heart of a person filled with the Holy Spirit. *This offering can be vocal, instrumental, or both together.* This conclusion is the result of much prayer and considerable study of the Scriptures on this matter.

. . . The conclusion of the FBCC leadership after much prayer and study is that *vocal and / or instrumental music is an acceptable expression of praise to the Lord. The leadership does not see this position standing in conflict with the Scriptures.* What is in conflict with them is that, for the sake of *maintaining a tradition,* FBCC quite possibly has put itself further out of touch with those whom it desires to touch the most, the unchurched of our culture. There can be no question that this was and is the top priority of Jesus, nor is there any question that He was constantly in conflict with the traditions of His day.

Because the purpose of the Farmers Branch Church is to accept people where they are and challenge them to grow in Christ, FBCC must take into consideration where the unchurched are in its attempt to meet them on common ground and lead them to holy ground. Music, specifically of the nature of instrumental accompaniment, is a common feature of life in our everyday culture. One doesn't turn on the radio and frequently hear a cappella songs, nor go to concerts, or listen to CDs and tapes featuring a cappella music. The scores and soundtracks to movies are rarely a cappella. When our culture thinks of "music" it automatically assumes songs with instrumental accompaniment. The musical form of a cappella is not something many in our culture are accustomed to listening to or appreciating[5] (emphasis added—dh).

EXPEDIENCY OR SALVATION?

Two striking things about the document stand out. The first is its utilitarian approach to the issue; that is, whatever works is best. The goal—according to the document—is to reach out to the masses, using what they are comfortable with. Second, instrumental music is in essence relegated to a matter of expediency—or, as the document claims, "not a salvation issue."

---

5. "A Consideration of Instrumental Accompaniment in Corporate Worship," Farmers Branch Church of Christ, not dated.

Related to the second point, the *Christian Chronicle* report quotes Rubel Shelly stating something he would not have said at one time:

> I am an unabashed defender of our a cappella legacy. But when someone wants me to go further and to condemn to hell someone who doesn't agree with my view, or to criticize congregations that choose to use instruments because they believe it will assist their outreach in a community different from mine, I have no interest in pursuing the discussion. Instrumental music and the atonement are not of the same status or consequence to the human soul and its eternal welfare.[6]

The claim that instrumental music is not a salvation issue is not new to Crystal Lake or to Rubel. In May 1999 *The Tennessean* reported that the Community Church of Christ in Hendersonville, Tennessee, introduced the instrument. As a result, its preacher was fired from Lipscomb, where he was on the faculty. Reporter Ray Waddle wrote:

> Weeks ago, according to some Community Church of Christ members, shepherds there announced to the congregation that the music question is not a "salvation" issue, so it's not important if the church adds instrumental music on occasion. There are more pressing concerns in the Christian life than the instrumental music issue, they suggested.[7]

KEEP THE YOUNG PEOPLE—BY USING THE INSTRUMENT?

One must consider also what the preacher for the Northwest congregation says. Milton Jones, in the book *The Transforming of a Tradition,* contributed a chapter entitled "The War Is Over." In it he compares the conflict in churches of Christ over instrumental music to the conflict over flying the Confederate flag in South Carolina and Georgia. He also describes the struggle within the Northwest congregation that ensued when the announcement was made of the leaders' intention to introduce the instrument. Jones's rationale, in part, was to keep the young people of the congregation. Instrumental music, he reasoned, would play a critical part. Jones continues:

---

6. Adams.

7. Ray Waddle, "Congregation's Use of Music Creates Echoes of Discord," *The Tennessean,* May 23, 1999.

When it comes to change, Churches of Christ are going to have to talk about the instrumental music issue. And we have to get past some of the emotions that we carry. It is as if we are still fighting the Civil War. And if you haven't noticed, the war is over.

When it comes to change, we need to change for the sake of the mission. We don't need to change simply for the sake of change. But if we are not reaching the world and there is a way to communicate God's grace to people today, shouldn't we openly discuss it? To win the world to Christ, we are going to have to allow some freedom, and we are not going to get our way on every issue.[8]

In commenting on this, Leroy Garrett went a step further. Garrett himself is a study in extremes. During the 1950s he advocated the anti position on located preachers and cooperation, yet just a few years later he was openly advocating open fellowship with the denominations. In his publication *Once More with Love,* Garrett wrote an article titled "We Must Talk about Instrumental Music." In it he primarily addresses those who wish to bring in the instrument. After listing the possible reasons "progressive" congregations do not introduce the practice, he says:

But hardly anyone is saying what we must start saying: *We have been wrong about instrumental music.* I am confident that that will be our conclusion once we broach the subject honestly.

We have not been wrong in being a cappella. All churches sometimes sing a cappella. Some of the great choirs are a cappella. Some of the oldest denominations have historically been a cappella, such as in the Orthodox tradition.

We have been wrong in that we have made the use of the instrument a test of fellowship. We have made our preference or opinion an essential to the faith. This is what we must confess and repudiate, even when we go right on being a cappella—as our own preference, while in brotherly love we recognize that others see it differently[9] (emphasis in original—dh).

In a later issue of the publication, he elaborates further:

Our position must now be that while for conscience' sake we will remain non-instrumental, we will no longer make it a test of fellowship. We are now to realize that instrumental music is an issue upon which Christians can differ and still be one in Christ. We can have "instru-

---

8. Milton Jones, "The War Is Over," in *The Transforming of a Tradition,* Leonard Allen & Lynn Anderson, eds. (Orange, CA: New Leaf, 2001), 83.

9. Leroy Garrett, "We Must Talk about Instrumental Music," *Once More with Love,* No. 51, (Oct. 2001), 1.

mental" churches and "non-instrumental" churches and still accept each other as equals. It is a matter of congregational preference. Some of us in Churches of Christ can even believe that for *us* to sing with instruments it would be a sin without insisting that it is a sin for others. We can even believe that we are closer to the spirit of the New Testament when we sing a cappella, as I believe, without rejecting those who differ with us.

The good news is that instrumental music is increasingly becoming a non-issue among us. But we must do more than this by being proactive in denouncing this sectarian dogma that has done so much harm for so long.[10]

SCRIPTURE AND HISTORY

Garrett's position on the subject is possibly the norm among the leaders of the New Left. They want the practice to be widely accepted among churches of Christ. They, like Garrett, are frustrated at the relatively few congregations that have incorporated the practice. They have the attitude described in the title of this chapter: "Instrumental Music Is Not a Salvation Issue—But We Will Have It, Regardless!"

But what should be our response? Is it the case that instrumental music is indeed not a salvation issue? May one choose to use it or not to use it and still be right in the sight of God? It is our contention that the music offered in worship (whether vocal or instrumental) does matter, and that it strikes to the very heart of the issue: respect for biblical authority.

In *Among the Scholars* I included a chapter on instrumental music. In it, it was demonstrated from the Scriptures how the practice is sinful. Those clamoring to introduce the practice have not answered the reasons given at that time. Indeed, those reasons are not original with me, but have been given by brethren for many generations. Neither could those in days gone by who wished to have the instrument successfully answer.

To summarize, the New Testament does not indicate—either by direct statement, apostolic example, or implication—that instrumental music is acceptable in worship. Additionally, the historical evidence is just as clear. The first successful introduction of the instrument into "Christian worship" was not until the tenth century—long after

---

10. Garrett, "What I Want for Churches of Christ," *Once More with Love,* No.56, (Aug. 2002), 1–2.

the apostolic age. The Greek word *psallo* means "I sing," and does not include the instrument in New Testament usage. Indeed, if it did include it, no Christian could obey Colossians 3:16 or Ephesians 5:19 without bringing and using his or her own instrument. Also, John 4:24 is a key passage: "God is a Spirit: and they that worship him must worship him in spirit and in truth." In this verse the object of our worship is God. The manner of our worship is "in spirit." The standard of our worship is "in truth." That is, our worship must be directed by the word of God.

One would be hard pressed to believe that pizza and Coca-Cola would be accepted in the Lord's supper among congregations of the Left. However, that which would allow the instrument also allows pizza and coke on the Lord's table. In fact, there is as much authority for counting beads and reciting the Catholic Rosary in prayer as there is to use the instrument—which is to say, there is no such authority.

TRUE DOCTRINE: TRUE WORSHIP

Colossians 3:17 is a verse that must not be ignored: "And whatsoever ye do in word or deed, do all in the name of the Lord Jesus, giving thanks to God and the Father by him." To do something in the name of someone means to do it by his authority. Can one truly say that instrumental music is according to God's authority? Matthew 15:9 says, "But in vain they do worship me, teaching for doctrines the commandments of men." This passage shows that true doctrine is connected to true worship.

First Samuel 15:13–15, 20–23 recites an incident that amplifies the danger of offering unauthorized worship:

> And Samuel came to Saul: and Saul said unto him, Blessed be thou of the Lord: I have performed the commandment of the Lord. And Samuel said, What meaneth then this bleating of the sheep in mine ears, and the lowing of the oxen which I hear? And Saul said, They have brought them from the Amalekites: for the people spared the best of the sheep and of the oxen, to sacrifice unto the Lord thy God; and the rest we have utterly destroyed . . . And Saul said unto Samuel, Yea, I have obeyed the voice of the Lord, and have gone the way which the Lord sent me, and have brought Agag the king of Amalek, and have utterly destroyed the Amalekites. But the people took of the spoil, sheep and oxen, the chief of the things which should have been utterly destroyed, to sacrifice unto the Lord thy God in Gilgal. And Samuel said, Hath the Lord as great delight in burnt

offerings and sacrifices, as in obeying the voice of the Lord? Behold, to obey is better than sacrifice, and to hearken than the fat of rams. For rebellion is as the sin of witchcraft, and stubbornness is as iniquity and idolatry. Because thou hast rejected the word of the Lord, he hath also rejected thee from being king.

Indeed, this principle—obeying the Lord—still holds true today. One does not have any right to alter God's Word to do what he wants in worship. John says, "Whosoever transgresseth, and abideth not in the doctrine of Christ, hath not God. He that abideth in the doctrine of Christ, he hath both the Father and the Son" (2 John 9).

But there are elderships that insist on their way—or no way. In September 1999, the Oak Hills Church of Christ—where Max Lucado preaches—issued this statement: "After many months of careful study and consideration, the elders unanimously concluded that there is no biblical prohibition of the use of mechanical instruments in worship."[11] What if an eldership were to announce that after many months of study and consideration, they concluded that there is no prohibition of praying to Mary. Would that make it right? To ask is to answer. There is as much biblical authority for one as there is for the other. No eldership has the right to set aside what the Scriptures teach on this or any other subject.

Disturbingly, though, there are those who have the attitude that the non-use of the instrument is simply a matter of tradition. This seems to be the attitude taken by Steve Flatt, former president of David Lipscomb University. In the aforementioned *Tennessean* article, he is quoted as saying:

> If Community church is going to be an instrumental congregation, that's not in accord with our policy . . . Our identity for the last 108 years has included a cappella . . . it still characterizes who we are . . . I don't know where Community Church of Christ is going—it's not my business. I don't run that congregation.[12]

To say this statement is a disappointment would be an understatement. Flatt had an excellent opportunity to explain the reasons why churches of Christ do not use the instrument, yet he chose not to take advantage of it. Contrast that with presidents of the past, who

---

11. Oak Hills Church of Christ worship bulletin, Sept. 5, 1999.
12. Waddle.

would not have shirked from explaining why the practice is unscriptural.

Instrumental music in worship is a salvation issue. It affects the unity of the local congregation, as well as the body of Christ as a whole. It undermines respect for the authority of the Word of God. It is unauthorized worship.

In 1860 Benjamin Franklin—the gospel preacher, not the statesman—wrote words that are just as appropriate today as they were when he originally penned them.

> Instrumental music is permissible for a church under the following conditions:
>
> 1. When a church never had or has lost the Spirit of Christ.
> 2. If a church has a preacher who never had or has lost the Spirit of Christ, who has become a dry, prosing and lifeless preacher.
> 3. If a church only intends being a fashionable society, a mere place of amusements and secular entertainment and abandoning the idea of religion and worship.
> 4. If a church has within it a large number of dishonest and corrupt men.
> 5. If a church has given up all idea of trying to convert the world.[13]

The instrumental music issue is important. It must be answered by all those who wish to preserve the unity of the body of Christ, based on truth. Jesus said, "If ye love me, keep my commandments" (John 14:15). We can do no less.

QUESTIONS FOR DISCUSSION

1. Is it remarkable that instrumental music is an issue today in churches of Christ? Defend your answer.

2. What is the real intent in saying that instrumental music is not "a salvation issue"?

3. Give some reasons why instrumental music is wrong.

---

13. Benjamin Franklin, *American Christian Review,* 1860.

CHAPTER SIX

What about Contemporary "Christian" Music?

In recent years, many people have chosen to listen to contemporary "Christian" music (CCM). Reacting against the excesses of popular music, some parents have gladly allowed their children to attend concerts, buy CDs, and support CCM artists. Indeed, when one listens to a CCM radio station, he is struck by how similar—at first blush— the music is with mainstream pop. In fact, one can hear every musical style represented. Several CCM artists have "crossed over" to succeed in the mainstream—Jars of Clay, Sixpence None the Richer, Amy Grant, and others come to mind.

The appeal of CCM is obvious. The lyrics to top CCM songs are not vulgar; they do not employ obscene language or focus on inappropriate themes. The performers—at least in public—advocate standards of morality compatible with the Bible. The environment of the concerts is far more family friendly than that of most mainstream acts. No wonder, then, that CCM has enjoyed recent success. Additionally, there are congregations that are clamoring to incorporate CCM into worship services—or, at least, CCM-inspired music. As we will see, however, there are serious concerns that the child of God must address.

Consider this report, about a Tampa Bay, Florida, CCM concert:

> From high above, they swarmed like an ocean of typical teenagers headed to an 'N Sync concert: they moved in packs. They chattered. They wore baggy jeans and baseball caps and carried cell phones. But at ground level, in the bustle Friday night outside the St. Pete Times Forum, the details told a different story.
>
> Their shirts bore slogans like "Stone Cold Dead without Jesus" and "God Squad" and "Angel." Many toted well-worn Bibles bound in leather. The vans they arrived in came from Winter Haven and Floral City and Seminole. Most had church logos on the sides, with crosses hand-painted in the windows.

Welcome to Christianity, MTV style.

The throngs came for the kickoff of "Acquire the Fire," a week-end-long gathering that mixes a rock concert atmosphere with a religious message. The rallies, part of the nonprofit Teen Mania ministry, began in 1991 and have grown steadily in popularity.

One reason might be because they provide something nearly every teen craves—acceptance.

"You don't have to feel embarrassed," said 16-year-old Seth Zipp of Bradenton. "There are thousands of more kids here worshiping, just like you."

That same feeling has drawn 17-year-old Catherine Campbell to the event for the past three years. "I feel like I'm not the only Christian teenager out here," said Campbell, who came with her youth group from Miami. "Every teenager you see here, they want to be here. [And] the people who are out on stage are our age. They can relate to us."

Even the youth leaders and gray-haired parents, knowing they would face six-foot tall speakers and electric guitars, seemed content in the sea of raucous teenagers.

"It's Friday night. These kids could be out on the corner doing drugs, but they're not," said 45-year-old Brian Pape of Dunedin, who came with his son's youth group. "This lets them see a different alternative. They're able to cut loose and be themselves."

On this night, the Outpost bar across from the Forum sat silent. The Bacardi Rum "Shots at Channelside" was closed. The vendors weren't selling beer.

But the crowds still came, more than 11,000 strong.

In the bowels of the Forum, Christian band members milled around back stage. Song lists and prayer lists hung on the walls, not far from a Zamboni.

Then smoke filled the stage. A drum beat shook the floor. An electric guitar rang out. Bodies swayed in the crowd.

And the lead singer stepped toward the microphone. Hallelujah! Hallelujah! he sang into the darkness.

The ocean of teenagers shouted back.

Hallelujah.[1]

THE HISTORY OF CCM

To understand CCM, one must know a bit about its history. CCM sprang out of traditional "Gospel" music, in part as a reaction to it.

---

1. Brady Dennis, "Teenagers Flock to Rock 'n' Religion," *St. Petersburg Times* Feb. 22, 2003, http://www.sptimes.com/2003/02/22/TampaBay/Teenagers_flock_to_ro.shtml.

"Gospel" grew out of the black spirituals of the nineteenth century, and evolved along with denominational trends. In the Deep South, white quartets—such as the Blackwood Brothers and the Jordanaires —came to typify the image most had of "Gospel" by the 1960s. Indeed, Elvis Presley used the Jordanaires as part of his backup ensemble. Black "Gospel" was exemplified by Kirk Franklin, James Cleveland, Shirley Caesar, and many others.

By the decade of the 1960s, "Gospel" music underwent a profound shift—not unlike what was taking place in the United States. David Wang succinctly captures the mood of the time:

> For anyone who lived through the '60s, it was a time of sex, drugs and rock and roll. Thus, the thought of anything resembling rock music being played in churches was too radical to consider. However, in the early '70s, a new phenomenon started in California. Some of the "hippie" generation caught on to Christianity and a new Jesus Movement was started. Small grassroots Charismatic churches were started by young Christians who adopted the long hair and lifestyle of their contemporaries but had a love and desire to follow Christ. They began to use rock music with Christian lyrics to reach their generation. Some of the fruits of this movement even had an impact on the secular scene with songs like "Spirit in the Sky" (Norm Greenbaum) and "Jesus Is Just Alright" (Doobie Brothers) hitting the airwaves.[2]

One must understand that when writers like Wang use terms such as *Christian,* they have an ecumenical meaning—that is, all denominations are right in God's sight. We will shortly see how this belief is one of the major problems with CCM.

Lisa Howell delves even deeper into the roots of CCM:

> Christian music, as we know it today, arose from a period in American history known as the Jesus Movement. It is difficult to pinpoint exactly when and how this movement got started, but many consider the opening of The Living Room in the Haight Ashbury district of San Francisco in 1967 to be the starting point. The Living Room was a sort of half-way house run by "Street Christians" (former drug addicts, hippies, and street walkers become Christians) to reach out to those who were in the same place they once were.

---

2. David Wang, "The History of Contemporary Christian Music," http://www.catholicrock.com/cath/cathregsept1.html.

The Jesus Movement was not generally accepted by the mainstream American church. The Jesus People were long-haired ex-drug addicts and hippies who still dressed and looked the same, so the people of the church saw no change in them. As Larry Norman said, they were "like books that don't seem to match their covers." Yet, "the miracle of salvation had set their souls on fire and they wanted to share it with their brothers and sisters." The Jesus People, or Jesus Freaks as they were also called, took the message of Christ to people who would not go to church, and who would not have been welcomed there. These were the very people that Jesus Himself went looking for: they were drug addicts, criminals, prostitutes, and runaways. Like Jesus, the Jesus People had a deep longing to reach the unlovable and unwanted of society.

This longing reached its obvious culmination in the advent of street preachers, underground newspapers, and Jesus Music. These began as an effort of these new Christians to reach their peers with the gospel. Though gospel music already existed in some forms, it was not what the people of the hippie generation wanted to hear, so the Jesus Musicians took the music they loved, which was rock and roll, and coupled it with lyrics about what was now the most important thing in their lives, Jesus Christ. Chuck Girard said it well when he wrote, "We didn't know much about what people called Gospel music, we were just writing the same kind of songs we would write if we weren't Christians, but now we had Jesus to sing about."[3]

By the late 1970s, performers such as Sandi Patty began to garner success, in part because of a more mainstream pop style. During the 1980s, the genre expanded to incorporate such acts as Petra, a band with a heavy rock edge, and Stryper, a group that mimicked heavy metal—not only in its style of music, but also in its choice of clothes and hairstyle. Even Bob Dylan recorded a couple of religious albums in the late '80s, enjoying critical acclaim.

The decade of the 1990s witnessed an explosion of styles within CCM. Artists such as The Winans, Steven Curtis Chapman, MXPX, DC Talk, and The Newsboys exemplified the diversity. There is now a CCM band representing almost every style of music, from pop, reggae and R&B, right down to swing, punk, and death metal. CCM concerts are almost commonplace in most towns. Even *Billboard* magazine

---

3. Lisa Howell, "The Rise of Contemporary Christian Music," December 2000, http://www.angelfire.com/ca2/frogprincess/frames/history/history.html.

has recognized the success of CCM, giving it equal status with pop, country, and rap.

Does It Matter?

That being said, CCM has its own set of problems. Although the songs are not vulgar, the overall message sent is not one in keeping with the truth of God's Word. CCM couches its music in the context of "worship and praise." Artists will often urge listeners and those in the audience of their concerts to "accept Jesus," and tout what they do as "a ministry."

Is what is taking place at such events acceptable in the sight of God? To answer the question, we need to look briefly at what worship involves. As we have previously seen, Jesus gave the clearest indication of such in John 4:24: "God is a Spirit: and they that worship him must worship him in spirit and in truth." In this verse, Jesus tells us that the object of our worship must be God, not ourselves. Remember, God is the audience—not us! The Lord then indicates that worship is not optional; He says we "must" worship God. Jesus goes on to tell us the attitude of our worship: "in spirit." Our hearts must be turned wholly upon God as we worship Him. Finally, Jesus informs us about the standard of our worship: "in truth." He would later pray, "Sanctify them through thy truth: thy word is truth" (John 17:17). All that we do must be in keeping with the Word of God.

In light of what the Son of God spoke, does "worship" at CCM events seem acceptable? Instrumental music is used freely. Does it matter what music we employ in worship? As we observed in the previous chapter, it matters to God, in spite of what many might say. In the New Testament the only kind of music for the church on earth to use is vocal—not instrumental. It is not a matter of what I might want, or what someone else might desire, but rather what God wants.

The Authority Principle

Colossians 3:16–17 says,

> Let the word of Christ dwell in you richly in all wisdom; teaching and admonishing one another in psalms and hymns and spiritual songs, singing with grace in your hearts to the Lord. And whatsoever ye do in word or deed, do all in the name of the Lord Jesus, giving thanks to God and the Father by him.

Verse 17 has been called the "authority principle" of the New Testament. To do something "in the name of" someone means to do it by that person's authority. Given the fact that those involved in CCM events will say they are doing things "in the name of Jesus," doesn't it stand to reason that the claim should be investigated in the light of Scripture? Instrumental music in worship fails miserably, no matter how much people may want it. I enjoy playing and singing with my family and friends; however, I cannot bring my bass guitar into any worship service, whether it be in a church building, a school auditorium, someone's private home, or a large amphitheater.

There are only two kinds of music people can make—vocal and instrumental. In the New Testament, there is no direct statement allowing instrumental music in worship on earth. In fact, as we have already indicated, all Scripture addressing the subject mentions only singing. Also, we have no recorded example in God's Word of any congregation or group of Christians ever using instruments in worship. Indeed, the first recorded case of such is not until A.D. 616. And then it was vigorously opposed. It was not successfully introduced until the tenth century! Finally, there is no implication of instrumental music being allowed by the inspired authors of the New Testament.

Some have claimed that instruments aid in worship, but are not essential, so we can use them to assist us. However, that argument ignores the fact that vocal and instrumental are two different kinds of music—God authorized vocal music; He did not authorize instrumental. For something to be an aid, it must first be allowed by God. That is, it must not change the nature of the thing being done. That is why pizza or coke on the Lord's table is not allowed. The Lord specified in the Gospel accounts, as well as Paul's inspired statements in 1 Corinthians 11, what we are to use on the table. He likewise specified singing. CCM assumes that using instruments in "worship" is approved by God. Those involved make it appear that He is very pleased with such. The evidence from the New Testament indicates clearly the opposite to be the case.

A LOOSE VIEW OF FELLOWSHIP

We need to be very careful, indeed, when we make claims that cannot be substantiated by the Bible. Young people—and older ones, for that matter—are attending CCM concerts and buying CDs, and are being influenced by such. Over-enthusiastic youth ministers and preachers encourage youth groups in this way, and thereby affect the congregation. In do doing, they prepare the congregation for the introduction of CCM-inspired worship songs.

CCM promotes a loose view of fellowship. The old saw, "We're all going to heaven; we're just traveling down different roads," is repackaged in a far more attractive way. However, Jesus did not promise to build denominations. He said, "Upon this rock, I will build my church" (Matthew 16:18). In Ephesians 4:4 Paul declared there is "one body." In Ephesians 1:22–23 he declared that the body is the church.

In Ephesians 4 Paul also says there is one God, one Lord, and one faith. What would you think if your preacher declared next Sunday that there are many gods that make up the one God, such as the gods of Hinduism or Buddhism? How would you react if he were to say that there are many lords that make up the one Lord, and were to list Buddha, Gandhi, and others? What if he were then to claim that there are many faiths that make up the one faith?

The same logic that says there are many bodies (denominations) that make up the one body of Ephesians 4 must also make the same claim for the rest of the "ones" in the same passage. If not, why not? When Paul says "one," he means one. Denominationalism was unknown in the first century, and when a situation arose at Corinth that threatened the unity of the church, Paul addressed it immediately:

> Now I beseech you, brethren, by the name of our Lord Jesus Christ, that ye all speak the same thing, and that there be no divisions among you; but that ye be perfectly joined together in the same mind and in the same judgment. For it hath been declared unto me of you, my brethren, by them which are of the house of Chloe, that there are contentions among you. Now this I say, that every one of you saith, I am of Paul; and I of Apollos; and I of Cephas; and I of Christ. Is Christ divided? Was Paul crucified for you? Or were ye baptized in the name of Paul? (1 Corinthians 1:10–13).

How similar this is to the current state of religion! The difference, though, is that Paul gave the solution to the problem before it developed any further, and the brethren at Corinth accepted it. Today most people ignore the full impact of what Paul wrote, assuming that

God approves of divided "Christendom." CCM feeds on this thought process.

And this is reflected in the mindset of some of the performers. Amy Grant is perhaps the most successful artist affiliated with CCM. She has crossed over into pop several times, including a mid-1980s duet with former Chicago lead singer Peter Cetera, "Next Time I Fall in Love," and her 1992 hit "Baby, Baby." What may not be as familiar, however, is her connection with churches of Christ. Grant's parents are members of a Nashville congregation, and she was reared in that environment. However, she later left the church and embraced denominationalism.

Associated Press reporter Jim Patterson wrote an article in the spring of 2002 that shed some light on Grant:

> Looking back at the hundreds of church services she attended as a child, Christian music star Amy Grant can't recall one sermon. It's the music that got to her.
>
> "I grew up in a family where we went to church every Sunday morning, every Sunday night, and every Wednesday night," said Grant, who has sold more than 22 million albums. "Even on vacation, we would find a church and go. I can't remember any sermons from when I was a kid. I memorized a few Bible verses. But the hymns were always there."
>
> On Legacy . . . Hymns & Faith, Grant's first new album in five years (except for a Christmas album), she revives old hymns such as "This Is My Father's World" and "Holy, Holy, Holy." Husband Vince Gill, a country star, helped her rearrange the songs.
>
> "These songs gave me a feeling of security, a feeling that there was an eternal plan in place and operating," Grant said. "As I grew up hearing all these songs, it helped me to understand I have a place in this plan. No one is insignificant." Grant grew up in Nashville, the daughter of a surgeon. Her family belonged to the Church of Christ, and the Southern congregations don't allow any choirs or instrumental music. "So if you didn't sing, there was no noise, period," Grant said.[4]

---

4. Jim Patterson, "Amy Grant Revives Old Hymns, Plans September Pop Album," *The Decatur Daily*, May 18, 2002.

What she said at the outset of the piece is typical of far too many today. Little or no emphasis is placed upon hearing and learning the truth. Rather, emotional stimulation takes its place. While Grant looked back with fondness upon the hymns themselves, she had little to say about her home congregation.

De-emphasizing the truth and stressing emotionalism lead many away from Christ, all the while thinking they are drawing closer to Him. How can one know he is following Jesus if he never takes the time to see what Jesus and His apostles said? Additionally, how can one be a true disciple of Jesus if he turns away from Jesus' body, the church?

Hostility towards the Church

How well I remember the excitement among some of my college classmates in the mid-1980s, when we learned of Grant's connection to the church. However, that favorable feeling was dulled by the revelation of her departure. Interestingly, to some of my classmates this did not matter—indeed, it seemed to enhance her stature. Such also seems to be the mind-set among some today.

Indeed, consider the hostility of one of the "pioneers" of CCM toward the concept of the church. Larry Norman was interviewed by CCM Magazine, and was asked, "What was your view of the church?" He replied:

> I had no time for the church matrix. I didn't think you needed a majority vote from the elders on the board to undertake a musical ministry. The churches weren't going to accept me looking like a street person with long hair and faded jeans. They did not like the music I was recording. And I had no desire to preach the gospel to the converted. I wanted to be out on the sidewalk preaching to the runaways and the druggies and the prostitutes.
>
> When non-believers used to criticize the church I would say, "Yeah, I agree and I think that God is disappointed in what people have done with Jesus." And then I would go on to talk about what Christ personally said and did. It worked. I wasn't there to argue against people's beliefs. I was there to talk about what God's truth is.[5]

---

5. Gregory Rumburg, "Rock for the Ages," *CCM Magazine.com,* http://www.ccmcom.com/features/858.aspx.

For all of the assumed attractiveness of CCM, even some in the denominational world are beginning to have doubts. *CCM Magazine* recently reported that the industry generates $450 million, making it one of the fastest growing areas of the music business. In 1999 alone, 50 million units were sold.[6] Several within the industry have spoken out against the commercialization of CCM, even though they have no problem with the message of the songs.

AFFAIRS AND BLASPHEMY

Some of the artists within CCM have done things that are little different from their counterparts in country, rock, and pop. Michael English confessed to an extra-marital affair with a backup singer within days of winning six Gospel Music Association Dove Awards in 1994. Sandi Patty sent shock waves throughout the industry when she revealed she had been involved in two adulterous relationships during the same time. And, of course, Amy Grant's saga with Vince Gill is still fresh on the minds of many.

Even so, the lyrics to some CCM songs are just as blasphemous as those that one would find on the Billboard Hot 100. Carman Dominic Licciardello, better known as Carman, is one of the most popular performers in CCM. His concerts are regularly sold out. However, consider this exchange between Jesus Christ and John the Baptist on Carman's video, "Live . . . Radically Saved":

> John: "Hey man, Hey cuz, Whatchoo doin', man? I ain't seen you in a long time. Hey, baby."
> Jesus turns and says, "Hey, what's up, John?" [Carman then has Jesus Christ doing what Carman calls "The Messiah Walk".]
> John: "This is wild, brother, now I don't know. Man, I never had anybody in my family make it big . . ."[7]

On Carman's video, "Resurrection Rap," the artist portrays Jesus as a confused street hippie, while the apostles are gang members. The crucifixion takes place in a back alley gang fight, and Jesus is

---

6. "Christian music moves against current to go mainstream," *CNN.com* December 14, 2000, http://www.cnn.com/2000/SHOWBIZ/Music/12/14/wb.christian/.

7. Terry Watkins, "Christian Rock: Blessing or Blasphemy?" http://www.av1611.org/crock.html.

buried in a garbage dumpster.[8] Such a blasphemous stunt could hardly have been pulled off better by an atheistic rock band. But there's more.

Carman recorded a song, "Who's in the House," that contains these blasphemous lyrics:

> Tell me who's in the house? J.C.
> Tell me who's in the house? J.C.
> Tell me who's in the house? J.C.
> Tell me who's in the house? J.C.
> Jesus Christ is in the house today."[9]

If that were not enough, consider his offering, "Holy Ghost Hop":

> Everybody used to do the twist,
> The mashed potato and it goes like this.
> The funky chicken, monkey too;
> There wasn't nothin' they would not do.
> But there's a new dance no one can stop;
> A leap for joy we call the Holy Ghost Hop.
> Now get ready, hold steady;
> Don't deny it, just try it,
> Be bold now, let it go now;
> Give the Holy Ghost control now.[10]

Lyrics that mock the Godhead are without divine approval. Of God, David wrote, "Holy and reverend is his name" (Psalm 111:9). John articulates the attitude that should characterize all people: "Who shall not fear thee, O Lord, and glorify thy name? For thou only art holy: for all nations shall come and worship before thee; for thy judgments are made manifest" (Revelation 15:4).

Additionally, dancing is not of God; it is of the world. No matter how clever the efforts may be to "Christianize" dancing, it is still related to lasciviousness—one of the works of the flesh listed in Galatians 5:19–21. Paul declared, "Of the which I tell you before, as I have also told you in time past, that they which do such things shall not inherit the kingdom of God." How can a child of God sanction such?

---

8. Ibid.
9. Ibid.
10. Ibid.

When all is said and done, CCM must be judged by the same standards as any other style of music—perhaps even by a stricter standard, given the claims that are made for its songs and performers. If we are to uphold the New Testament as our only rule of faith and practice, and the Lord's church as the one body for which Jesus died, then CCM must be held accountable for what it promotes and teaches through its music. Certainly, Christians must give CCM a long, hard look before endorsing it—much less, supporting it by paying for CDs or concerts, or incorporating it into worship, which would be violating God's Word. If we are to be the people God wants us to be, we can do no less.

QUESTIONS FOR DISCUSSION

1. Given the origins of CCM, is it possible for the truth to be promoted in its songs? Defend your answer.

2. Examine again the statement quoted from the "Soulstock" Web site on "I Want to Be a Christian." Can a child of God defend such from the New Testament?

3. Does the use of instrumental music in CCM matter? Defend your answer.

4, Is the fellowship question in CCM significant for Christians? Defend your answer.

5. Does Carman's song, "Who's in the House," promote reverence for Jesus?

CHAPTER SEVEN

The Holy Spirit, Pope Benedict XVI, and the New Left

On April 19, 2005, the Roman Catholic Church chose Joseph Ratzinger to succeed John Paul II as its Pope. Upon selection, Ratzinger selected the name "Benedict XVI" to designate himself. The reaction to the announcement was interesting, to say the least. NewsMax.com reporter Phil Brennan wrote:

> When friends asked former U.S. Ambassador to the Vatican Raymond Flynn who would be the new pope, he told me that he answered that while he guessed Cardinal Ratzinger would be chosen, that was up to the most influential figure who would be present at the conclave. "When they asked me who that was," he said, "I told them 'the Holy Spirit.' "[1]

Flynn's take was not unique to him. Theresa Huntenburg, writing in *The Florida Catholic,* quoted a parishioner at a Pensacola area Catholic church: "I think he will make a very good pope and I pray that the Holy Spirit guides him to bring Jesus to the world."[2]

Writing in *The Catholic Standard & Times,* Christie L. Chicoine quoted Auxiliary Bishop Michael F. Burbidge as accurately predicting the selection of Ratzinger. He then said: "Even before that curtain opened today, no matter who came out [onto the balcony], I believed it was the Holy Spirit guiding the universal Church."[3] Later in the same article, Burbidge states: "We've been given by the gift of the

---

1. Phil Brennan, "Habemus Papam," *NewsMax.com* April 20, 2005, http://newsmax.com/archives/articles/2005/4/19/202720.shtml.
2. Theresa Huntenburg, "Catholics celebrate election of Pope Benedict XVI," *The Florida Catholic* April 20, 2005, http://www.thefloridacatholic.org/articles/050429/050429-pt-pb16.htm.
3. Christie L. Chicoine, "'Pope Benedict XVI, we love you!'" *The Catholic Standard & Times,* http://www.cst-phl.com/050421/second.html.

Holy Spirit a real Churchman, a loyal bishop and priest," one who is a "strong defender of the truth. We will be well served."[4]

Speaking of the 115 cardinals who selected Ratzinger, Brennan wrote: "They went into the conclave prayerfully, leaving themselves open to the guidance of the Holy Spirit. They got it in a hurry."[5]

He further asserts,

> A couple of years ago, for example, Cardinal Ratzinger asked Pope John Paul II to allow him to retire. He was tired and wanted to go home to Bavaria. The pope, obviously inspired by the Holy Spirit—who we now know had other plans for the cardinal—said no, so Cardinal Ratzinger stayed.[6]

Brennan closed his column in a similar vein: "We have a new pope, and we still have the Holy Spirit guiding him and our Church and the rest of us through these perilous times. (He even helps some columnists, who couldn't do it without His help, write their columns.)"[7]

However, it was not just overtly Catholic sources attributing Ratzinger's selection to the third person of the Godhead. *Fox News* seemed overnight to transform itself into "The Pope Channel," with fawning reporters and uncritical analysis of the process and procedure, and in so doing disappointing millions of viewers who expected better. The day of Ratzinger's selection, a reporter asked two young seminary students what they thought. They attributed his selection to the Holy Spirit. Additionally, FoxNews.com quoted Thomas Weber, 22, of Hettange, France: "I didn't care who it was, because he is guided by the Holy Spirit."[8]

As for the newly installed Pope, he delivered his first sermon not long after his appointment. According to *Catholic News,* the third person of the Godhead was also on his mind:

> Pope Benedict discussed "the happy coincidence between Pentecost and the priestly ordinations [which] invites me to underscore the indissoluble tie that exists, in the Church, between the Spirit and the institution."
>
> "I referred to this last Saturday when I took possession of the chair of the bishop of Rome at St. John Lateran. The chair and the Spirit are intimately linked in reality, as are the charism and the

---

4. Ibid.

5. Brennan.

6. Ibid.

7. Ibid.

8. "Crowds Cheer Pope Benedict XVI," *FoxNews.com,* http://www.foxnews.com/story/0,2933,153883,00.html.

ordained ministry. Without the Holy Spirit the Church would be reduced to a merely human organization, weighed down by her very structures."

"But in turn, in the plans of God," he said, "the Spirit habitually uses human mediation to act in history. Precisely for this reason, Christ, Who constituted His Church on the foundation of the Apostles gathered around Peter, also enriched her with the gift of His Spirit so that, over the centuries. He could comfort her and lead her to the full truth."

In closing, the Pope asked that the ecclesial community would "remain always open and docile to the action of the Holy Spirit in order to be among men a credible sign and effective instrument of God's action!"[9]

What does this have to do with the New Left in churches of Christ? More than one might at first realize. When attention is paid to statements, books, and Web sites produced by those on the Left, it is evident that similar things are being said concerning the Holy Spirit. Of course, this would fall right in line with the ecumenical tendencies of the movement. One way to have open fellowship with the denominations is to express similar beliefs on the Holy Spirit.

This is seen in the language that is used by some congregations on their Web pages. The Oak Hills congregation in San Antonio, Texas, is one such example. Under the heading "Our Vision and Beliefs," the following assertion is made: "The Holy Spirit gives believers spiritual gifts (talents or abilities) (1 Corinthians 12:7–11; Romans 12:4–8) to be used to help others."[10]

Further, under the heading "Ministry Mission Statement," one finds this statement: "The Oak Hills Praise and Worship Ministry exists to enable all worshipers to have a heart-changing encounter with God the Father, in the presence of Jesus the Son, through the power of the Holy Spirit."[11]

A STEP FURTHER

Further, it is not just west of the Mississippi River where these kinds of statements are made. The Web site of the Otter Creek Church

---

9. "Pope stresses link between institution and Spirit," *Catholic News* May 17, 2005, http://www.cathnews.com/news/505/92.php.

10. http://oakhillschurchsa.org/about/vision/.

11. http://www.oakhillschurchsa.org/ministries/praiseandworship/.

of Christ in Nashville, Tennessee, seems to go a step further. Under the heading "Our Faith," one can read this:

> The Holy Spirit is completely God and does the work of the Father and Son. He teaches, gives gifts, and transforms us back into God's image.
>
> There is one Church. She is the community of people who have trusted in Jesus to satisfy God's justice for their own rebellion and to send the Holy Spirit to draw them closer to God and to make them more like God.
>
> God has given His church special ways in which we can draw close to Him personally and enjoy His blessings. These include baptism, prayer, worship, preaching, Bible study, gifts, fasting, and communion with Him.[12]

Thus, the idea is promoted, whether intentional or unintentional, that the miraculous gifts of the first century are available for Christians today. How different are the above citations from any mainline denominational Web site or, for that matter, from any creed or confession of faith? One would be hard pressed to show a major difference.

Certain preachers within churches of Christ have contributed to the murkiness of thought and understanding related to the subject of how the Holy Spirit works. Terry Rush, in his book, *The Holy Spirit Makes No Earthly Sense,* writes: "I am thoroughly persuaded that the Scriptures become nothing more than a book of 'blah' if we are not Spirit-led."[13] Consider also what Joe Beam says in his sermon "Discovering the Power of the Holy Spirit": "The Holy Spirit speaks through the Word, through wisdom, and through awakenings and promptings."[14]

The Jerusalem Meeting of Acts 15

During the 1996 Nashville Jubilee, Beam uttered additional observations that hearken more to neo-Pentecostalism than to the New Testament. He asserted that "the Holy Spirit of God speaks to us not just through the Bible," and attempted to make a case for the

---

12. http://www.ottercreek.org/about_faith.php.
13. http://members.aol.com/getwellcc/article0238.html.
14. Ibid.

Holy Spirit directly working today separate from the Word—by anecdotal evidence. He cited the Jerusalem meeting at Acts 15 as an example.

> The apostles and elders met to consider this question. After much discussion, Peter got up and addressed them: Brothers, you know that some time ago God made a choice among you that the Gentiles might hear from my lips the message of the gospel and believe.
>
> He's referring, of course, back to what happened in Acts chapters 10 and 11, the conversion story of Cornelius. And he goes on telling what God had done. In verse 8: "God, who knows the heart, showed that he accepted them by giving the Holy Spirit to them, just as he did to us." And of course on that occasion the Holy Spirit came before immersion. God obviously was making a very important point there. And he talks about that for a while.
>
> Verse 12: "The whole assembly became silent as they listened to Barnabas and Paul telling about the miraculous signs and wonders God had done among the Gentiles through them." Now, so far, basically what you have, at least that's recorded, is what we would today call anecdotal evidence. They're not referring back to scripture. They're referring to what has occurred. Peter says, "Here's what we saw." Paul says, "Here's what we saw."[15]

Thus, according to Beam, we today may refer to anecdotal evidence—"here is what we saw"—as proof of direct operation of the Holy Spirit today. However, as we shall see, significant differences abound.

> Now James says, "Let's compare what's happening to the Bible. Let's see if this that's happening is in contradiction to the word or in harmony to the word." Now, when they look at it they find that what is happening is not in contradiction to the word but is in harmony to the word and they're now trying to make a decision what they should do . . . "It is my judgment therefore that we should not make it difficult for the Gentiles who are turning to God . . . Then the apostles and elders with the whole church decided to choose some of their own men and send them back to Antioch with Paul and Barnabas. Now, they write a letter . . . and in verse 28 they say this in the letter: "It seemed good to the Holy Spirit and to us not to burden you with anything beyond the following requirements . . . This is our judgment." And when they came together in that judgment, they say it is good to the Holy Spirit. Now, if you read

---

15. Joe Beam, Tape 2, "The Holy Spirit," Nashville Jubilee, 1996.

that, they just ascribed their decision to the Holy Spirit. They gave him the credit for what they decided.[16]

What we actually have in Acts 15 is an account of inspired men meeting under the direct guidance of the Holy Spirit, not a modern-day "Holy Ghost miracle service." The apostles could verify their claims by the miracles they performed (Mark 16:20). No one today can make that claim. Paul demonstrated the truth of his claims by the miracles he did (2 Corinthians 12:12). Acts 15 is not, as Beam claims, an example of how people today can acquire spiritual wisdom separate and apart from the Word.

GOD'S "ONGOING ACTIVITY"

Another who pushes the idea that miracles still take place today, as they did in the first century, is Edward Fudge. Through his Web site, Fudge sets forth the notion that the age of miracles has not ceased. Fudge stands as a microcosm of what has taken place in churches of Christ. His father, the late Bennie Lee Fudge, was a prominent preacher among the "antis" of northern Alabama; he started CEI Bookstore in Athens, Alabama. Edward Fudge was prominent for a time among the non-cooperation wing, but broke with them when his leftist views began to come to the fore. Fudge wrote a book, *The Fire That Consumes,* in which he declared that hell is not a place of eternal punishment. Not long after, he moved to Texas, where he affiliated with the Bering Drive congregation in Houston. Bering Drive promotes a wide role for women, including leadership in worship and teaching mixed adult classes.

On his Web site, Fudge includes a multi-part series entitled "Miracles Still Happen." He says,

> Church history is replete with such occurrences until the period of the secularization, institutionalization, and sacramentalization of the Church in the fifth century. Credible reports of such mighty acts of God ("miracles" and "signs") abound today, for those who have not decided beforehand that such do not exist.[17]

Fudge further said, "According to the New Testament, God's ongoing activity in the world actually helps us rightly interpret the

---

16. Ibid.
17. http://www.edwardfudge.com/gracemails/supernatural_natural.html.

Scriptures"[18] (John 5:39–40; Acts 15:5–21). But in the passage from John, Jesus is upbraiding the Pharisees because they refused to see Him in Scripture; Jesus was personally with them, performing miracles. Neither Jesus, the apostles, nor anyone else is alive today performing miracles. As we have already seen, the Acts passage describes a meeting that cannot be duplicated today, because there are no apostles alive today. What we do have is the Spirit-inspired Word.

> And many other signs truly did Jesus in the presence of his disciples, which are not written in this book: but these are written, that ye might believe that Jesus is the Christ, the Son of God; and that believing ye might have life through his name (John 20:30–31).

"Broaden the Promise"

Fudge asserts, "The most natural reading of Acts 1–2 strongly suggests that the outpouring or baptism of the Holy Spirit at Pentecost included the whole company of believers in Jesus, not only the Apostles."[19] On the contrary, the "most natural reading" is conclusive that the twelve were the only ones baptized with the Holy Spirit. Acts 1:26 reads, "And they gave forth their lots; and the lot fell upon Matthias; and he was numbered with the eleven apostles." The next verse says, "And when the day of Pentecost was fully come, they were all with one accord in one place" (Acts 2:1). It is a basic rule of English, as well as Greek, that a pronoun agrees with its nearest antecedent. The antecedent of "they" in Acts 2:1 is "Matthias . . . with the eleven apostles" of Acts 1:26.

Further, Acts 2:7 specifies they were all Galileans who were filled with the Holy Spirit. Acts 2:13 reads, "Others mocking said, These men are full of new wine." Acts 2:14 says, "Peter, standing up with the eleven," not the one hundred twenty of Acts 1:15. Acts 2:37 asserts, "Now when they heard this, they were pricked in their heart, and said unto Peter and to the rest of the apostles, Men and brethren, what shall we do?" They did not address the 120. In attempting to broaden the promise Jesus made to the apostles, Fudge ignores plain Scripture.

---

18. Ibid.
19. http://edwardfudge.com/written/pentecosttext.html.

One other aspect of Fudge's Web site is interesting. He includes "A Service of Prayer for Christian Healing." In it Fudge outlines how such a service could be conducted—with responsive prayers and suggestions for songs and scriptures. Toward the end of the service, he includes an "Invitation for Anointing with Oil." Fudge suggests:

> Elders/pastors anoint each person in turn with oil (perhaps making sign of the Cross on forehead with finger or thumb dipped in olive or other oil), and, while laying hands on head or shoulder, pray specifically for divine healing for that individual.[20]

Fudge's "Service of Prayer for Christian Healing" is one that has no power, because the Holy Spirit no longer performs miracles today, as He did in the first century. When Fudge, Beam, or anyone else can restore lost limbs, restore sight to the blind, and raise the dead, then we will believe him. However, we are not waiting with bated breath.

THE HOLY SPIRIT WORKS THROUGH THE WORD

How does the Holy Spirit work today? How does He guide the child of God? Does He do anything to the child of God, separate and apart from the Word? In answering, we must first realize that He works now through God's spiritual law, God's Word. The Spirit works through the Word in the conviction and conversion of sinners (John 16:7–13). If God sent the Holy Spirit upon one sinner apart from the Word to convert him, then He would have to send the Holy Spirit upon all sinners to convert them or God would be a respecter of persons (Romans 2:11; Acts 10:34–35). If the Holy Spirit came upon the sinner separate and apart from the Word to convert him, it would make man a mere machine, and the gospel would not be God's power unto salvation (Romans 1:16; James 1:21). The Word, not a direct operation of the Holy Spirit, is the seed of the kingdom; not a direct operation of the Holy Spirit (Luke 8:11).

Second, the Holy Spirit works through the Word in leading Christians (Romans 8:13–14).

- He warns Christians through the Word as He did Israel (Neh. 9:20, 30).

- If the Holy Spirit gave any leadings other than through the Word of God, it would mean that the Scriptures are not sufficient "that

---

20. http://edwardfudge.com/written/healingservicetext.html.

the man of God may be perfect, throughly furnished unto all good works" (2 Timothy 3:16–17; 2 Peter 1:3).

Third, consider this: everything the Holy Spirit does to the child of God, the Word also does.

- The Spirit gives life (2 Corinthians 3:6); the Word gives life (James 1:18).

- Sinners are born again by the Spirit (John 3:8); sinners are born again by the Word (1 Peter 1:23–25).

- We are saved by the Spirit (Titus 3:5); we are saved by the Word (James 1:21).

- We are sanctified by the Spirit (1 Corinthians 6:11; 2 Thessalonians 2:13); we are sanctified by the word (John 17:17).

- We are led by the Spirit (Romans 8:14); we are led by the Word (Psalms 25:5; 43:3).

The Holy Spirit works now through God's natural laws in what He does for the child of God. He renews the face of the earth through nature. "Thou sendest forth thy spirit, they are created; and thou renewest the face of the earth" (Psalm 104:30). He creates people today by natural law. "The Spirit of God hath made me and the breath of the Almighty giveth me life" (Job 33:4).

The Spirit and the Word are inseparable in connection with what He does to the child of God, because the Word is the sword of the Spirit (Ephesians 6:17; Hebrews 4:12). We are not saying that the Word *is* the Spirit; all we are saying is that the Spirit operates on the hearts of alien sinners and Christians by means of the Word.

There is a big difference in saying what the Spirit does *for* the Christian and what the Spirit does *to* the Christian. The former is accomplished by providence; the latter is done through the Word.

WHAT GUS NICHOLS *REALLY* TAUGHT

One final point must be emphasized. Often those who advocate a semi-direct operation of the Holy Spirit upon the child of God—those who promote "promptings," or "urgings"—will claim they are simply taking Gus Nichols' position on the Holy Spirit. They will say that the disagreement over how the Spirit works is parallel to the disagreement between brother Nichols and brother Guy N. Woods over the indwelling of the Spirit. Is this the case?

The Bible affirms the fact that the Holy Spirit dwells in all Christians (Romans 8:9–11; 1 Corinthians 6:19–20; Galatians 4:6). This is sometimes called the "ordinary measure" of the Spirit. This measure of the Holy Spirit is not the baptism of the Holy Spirit; neither does it give miraculous power as the measure that was given by the laying on of the apostles' hands. Contrary to what the brethren on the Left contend, the Holy Spirit gives no extra leadings today apart from the Word of God.

Second, there are two positions taken by brethren concerning how the Holy Spirit indwells the Christian. Gus Nichols, in his outstanding book *Lectures on the Holy Spirit,* put forward the position that the Holy Spirit personally indwells the child of God. Brother Nichols pointed out that the Bible teaches clearly that we all have a soul, or spirit, dwelling in our bodies. We cannot prove it by feelings; only by the Bible. He then said that the Bible clearly teaches that the Holy Spirit dwells in the Christian. We cannot prove it by our feelings; only by the Bible.

Brother Nichols taught that the "gift of the Holy Spirit" in Acts 2:38 is the personal indwelling of the Spirit. Acts 5:32 was also stressed. He also stressed that the indwelling does not do anything to the child of God, nor can it be perceived with our five senses. An important point to emphasize: Brother Nichols went out of his way to stress that the Spirit works in salvation and sanctification only through the Word of God. Over and again in his book, he hammers this home. Those on the Left who claim to hold brother Nichols' position on the work of the Holy Spirit obviously have never read his book. They teach that the Holy Spirit operates directly on the child of God in a semi-miraculous way, giving leadings, promptings, or urgings separate and apart from the Word. This, brother Nichols never believed nor taught!

GUS NICHOLS AND GUY N. WOODS AGREED
ON THE WORK OF THE HOLY SPIRIT

Guy N. Woods, in his marvelous book *Questions and Answers: Open Forum,* put forward the position that the Holy Spirit indwells the child of God through, or by means of, the Word of God. Brother Woods affirmed that the Scriptures plainly teach that the Father (2 Corinthians 6:16; 1 John 4:12–16) and Christ the Son (Colossians 1:27) are in us. He further affirmed that both God and Christ dwell in our hearts by faith (Ephesians 3:17; John 14:23). Brother Woods then pointed to Galatians 3:2 as the text that indicates how the Holy Spirit indwells the child of God: "This only would I learn of you, Received ye the Spirit by the works of the law, or by the hearing of faith?" He also stressed the parallel between Ephesians 5:18, "Be filled with the Spirit," and Colossians 3:16, "Let the word of Christ dwell in you richly." As Woods asserted, "No one will be so foolish as to charge Paul with teaching that the Spirit and the Word are the same. Why then should we, when we assert that the Spirit dwells in the heart through, or by means of, the Word, be thus charged?" Brother Woods stressed, as did brother Nichols, that the Holy Spirit works in salvation and sanctification only through the Word of God.

Although brother Nichols and brother Woods disagreed over the question of how the Spirit indwells the child of God, they never allowed it to become a test of fellowship. The reason? Because they agreed on how the Spirit works—through the Word of God. They both rejected modern-day Pentecostalism and affirmed what the Scriptures plainly teach.

Brother Woods for many years was the moderator of the annual Open Forum at Freed-Hardeman. Brother Nichols often came to the podium with brother Woods to answer certain questions. Invariably, the question of the indwelling of the Spirit would be raised. Brother Woods would answer the question, and then from the audience brother Nichols would slowly arise and make his way to the podium, with titters and laughter from the audience—and with a smile on the face of both brother Nichols and brother Woods! Brother Nichols would then calmly affirm his position, and assert how that he had the utmost respect for brother Woods, and counted him as a faithful brother in Christ. Brother Woods would reciprocate, and they would—in good humor—go back and forth on the question. All present were impressed with the depth of biblical knowledge and sweet Christian spirit that existed between these two spiritual giants.

THE WORD IS COMPLETE

The attitude of brother Woods and brother Nichols needs to be restored within the body of Christ over matters of indifference! They saw the question of how the Spirit indwells as a matter of expediency. They followed Romans 14 on this matter, as well as many others. We would do well to follow their example. My grandfather, S. F. Hester, also disagreed with brother Nichols over how the Spirit indwells, but they never allowed it to come between them, because they also agreed on how the Spirit works.

Our brethren on the Left either fail to see the difference or are deliberately obfuscating the issue. The question of how the Spirit works today is not a matter of indifference, like the question of the indwelling—it is a matter of faith. The Word of God is complete in that it furnishes the man of God in every good work (2 Timothy 3:16–17; 2 Peter 1:3). To affirm otherwise is to deny the all-sufficiency of Scripture.

That brings us back to the original point. The position advocated by Pope Benedict XVI and denominational preachers is no different from what our brethren on the Left are advocating concerning how the Spirit works today. Our response must be firm, resolute, and from the Scriptures. Yes, the Spirit is working today—in the way that God has said!

QUESTIONS FOR DISCUSSION

1. Do Pope Benedict XVI and the Roman Catholics quoted advocate a position concerning the Holy Spirit that is substantially different from the New Left?

2. When congregations affirm that the Holy Spirit "gives gifts" today and then cite 1 Corinthians 12:7–11 as proof, what impression does that leave regarding the availability of miraculous gifts today?

3. Joe Beam claims that "anecdotal evidence" can be used to prove miracles happen today. If that is true, how can Christians deal with the claims of Pat Robertson and others like him?

4. Do you accept the position of brother Nichols or the position of brother Woods regarding the indwelling of the Spirit? Why?

CHAPTER EIGHT

Restoration or Revisionist History?

When I wrote *Among the Scholars* in 1994, one of the points made was that the New Left often engages in revisionist history; that is, a rewriting of what actually happened in the Restoration Movement. This is not substantially different from what the political Left has attempted to do with American History—or with Communism.

John Earl Haynes and Harvey Klehr co-authored *The Secret World of American Communism* and *Venona: Decoding Soviet Espionage*, both published by Yale University Press as part of its *Annals of Communism* series. Haynes and Klehr relied upon newly opened Soviet archives to paint a clear picture of the true nature of communist infiltration in the U.S. during the 1930s–40s. They also revealed recent declassified documents that detail how U.S. intelligence for a time decoded Soviet messages and how it shed light on some of the "unanswered" questions of the Cold War.[1]

Yet, regardless of the credentials of Haynes and Klehr (much less that of Yale University), those on the Left would have none of it. The revisionists either ignored the evidence or tried to minimize its importance. They also insisted that those who were guilty of espionage —Julius and Ethel Rosenberg, Alger Hiss, Harry Dexter White and others—were the victims of witch hunts. In so doing, the revisionists were still attempting to whitewash Stalin's regime and its American supporters.

---

1. Harvey Klehr, John Earl Haynes, and Fridikh Igorevich Firsov, *The Secret World of American Communism* (New Haven: Yale University Press, 1995); John Earl Haynes and Harvey Klehr, *Venona: Decoding Soviet Espionage in America* (New Haven: Yale University Press, 1999).

Haynes and Klehr wrote about their experience with the revisionists:

> We believe that some academics, including several prominent and influential ones, have written bad history in the service of bad politics. Their political enthusiasms have distorted their professional vision to the detriment of the historical profession and the search for truth about the past.[2]

Such could be said about the revisionists in the Lord's church.

A DISTORTED VISION

In 1996 Richard Hughes of Pepperdine University penned *Reviving the Ancient Faith: The Story of Churches of Christ in America.* Aside from the presumptuous claim of the title, his work does the brotherhood an unwitting service: it chronicles the history of radicalism within the Lord's church, all the way from the premillennial heresy of the 1930s to the current New Left movement. In addition, Hughes "connects the dots" in that he demonstrates the connections that exist between them.

It was one aspect of the book, though, that immediately caught my attention. In his 448-page work, Hughes devoted three chapters to the decade of the 1960s! Just in case anyone missed his point, though, Hughes had this to say:

> The protests of the younger generation among Churches of Christ *significantly paralleled* the protests of America's larger youth counterculture . . . young people among Churches of Christ charged their elders with having betrayed the ideals of their religious heritage (emphasis mine).

He also makes this preposterous claim: "The mainstream leadership had become liberal, and their children were the true conservatives."[3]

Another book that came from the opposite end of the spectrum was published by the University of Alabama in 2000. David Edwin Harrell Jr., a history professor at Auburn University, penned *The Churches of Christ in the 20th Century: Homer Hailey's Personal*

---

2. Haynes & Klehr, *In Denial: Historians, Communism and Espionage* (San Francisco: Encounter Books, 2003), 8.
3. Richard T. Hughes, *Reviving The Ancient Faith: The Story of Churches of Christ in America* (Grand Rapids: Eerdmans, 1996), 308.

Journey of Faith. Aligned with the non-cooperation brethren, Harrell also unwittingly does a useful service for faithful brethren. Writing from the "anti" perspective, Harrell fills in the blanks concerning radicalism in the church. In fact, he spends 137 pages addressing the division that ensued in the 1950s–60s, as well as the current controversy.[4] Harrell says virtually the same thing that Hughes does. Indeed, Hughes endorses the book enthusiastically on the dust jacket. This simply buttresses the point that the extreme Right and extreme Left dovetail; they come from the same destructive mind-set.

Communism and the Scholars Conference—A Coincidence?

Although those works in themselves validate my thesis, there remains one unanswered question: where did the organizers of the Christian Scholars Conference get the idea to launch such an event twenty years ago? The answer has finally come from a totally unexpected source. In 2001 Ronald Radosh, a founding father of the political New Left, published his memoir, *Commies: A Journey through the Old Left, the New Left and the Leftover Left*. Radosh, like Peter Collier and David Horowitz before him, has since become a conservative and renounced his radical past. His book provides some fascinating reading.

However, one passage toward the end of the book leaped off the page. After describing his efforts with other Leftists to form a new socialist party in the late 1960s, Radosh pens this amazing passage:

> We did, however, manage to create the intellectual group we named the *Socialist Scholars Conference*. The purpose of the organization was to create an atmosphere in which socialist scholarship would be taken seriously, and in which Marxists in the academy could show that they were producing work of merit that had a role to play in the intellectual marketplace."[5]

He then goes on to describe the second and third meetings of the SSC, and how the participants had their papers published. The

4. David Edwin Harrell, Jr., *The Churches of Christ in the 20th Century: Homer Hailey's Personal Journey of Faith* (Tuscaloosa, AL: University of Alabama Press, 2000), 39–176.
5. Ronald Radosh, *Commies: A Journey Through the Old Left, the New Left and the Leftover Left* (San Francisco: Encounter Books, 2001).

conclusions are all too easy to draw. It seems too obvious to be true, but it is surely more than coincidence that the CSC and the SSC not only had similar names but also similar meetings.

A BLATANT REVISION

One clear-cut instance of revisionism can be found from a book that is highly regarded by the New Left. In 1994 Douglas A. Foster, now professor at Abilene Christian University, wrote *Will the Cycle Be Unbroken?: Churches of Christ Face the 21st Century.* Much could be said about the book's assumptions and semantic games, but one point in particular bears scrutiny. Foster quotes from the late G. C. Brewer in support of an argument he makes concerning churches of Christ.

To understand the quotation, consider what Foster says just before it:

> On the other hand, to those who see Churches of Christ as a body of people dedicated to following Christ, but not the only ones legitimately making that effort, the above viewpoint [i.e. denying there are Christians "outside our borders"—dh] appears to be the ultimate example of sectarianism. This second group agrees wholeheartedly that Christ's church encompasses all the saved and that it is not a denomination. They insist, however, that Christ's church is not confined to one visible, historically-bound body named Churches of Christ. Both sides condemn sectarianism, but each holds a radically different concept of what it is.[6]

Foster continues, "There have always been respected voices in Churches of Christ who have insisted that neither biblical Christianity nor our immediate heritage were exclusive in nature."[7] Notice the word *exclusive.* He then says, "Doctrinally conservative and loyal to Churches of Christ, these voices have insisted that the bounds of God's family are not confined to our fellowship."[8] Note that quotation well. It will loom in importance shortly.

---

6. Douglas A. Foster, *Will the Cycle Be Unbroken? : Churches of Christ Face the 21st Century* (Abilene, TX: ACU Press, 1994), 48–49.

7. Ibid.

8. Ibid.

Foster proceeds to quote from brother Brewer. As laid out in Foster's book, it reads:

> Any institution that does not include all of God's creation cannot be the church of God. Even if such an institution is composed entirely of Christians, contains only Christians, and yet does not contain all Christians, it cannot be the church of God . . . To apply the terms *the church,* or the church of God or the church of Christ to any limited number of Christians is to sectarianize these scriptural phrases . . . We have, in spite of ourselves, become a sect whose special purpose it is to contend against sectarianism (emphasis Foster's).[9]

SCRUTINIZING FOSTER'S CONTENTION

At first glance, brother Brewer seems to support Foster's contention. However, two things immediately come to mind. First, what did Foster omit from the citation? Considering his track record—attributing the words of a Baptist preacher to David Lipscomb in the inaugural issue of *Wineskins* magazine—suspicions would naturally arise. Second, consider what Foster said immediately preceding the citation: "People like G. C. Brewer (d. 1956) and Monroe Hawley have insisted that we cannot and must not equate our visible fellowship of Churches of Christ, as great and noble as it is, with the universal church."[10] Could that be what Brewer was saying?

In checking the quotation, one finds that it is from the 1952 Harding lectures. Brewer's lecture was titled, "The New Testament Church and Sectarianism." In searching for the lectureship book, I discovered that it is hard to find. But in a moment of sweet irony, the Abilene Christian University library had a copy and lent it!

When Brewer's lecture is read in full, the two concerns just mentioned are validated. The first three sentences of the citation by Foster are from page 165 of Brewer's lecture in a section titled, "Whom Does the Church Include?" After pointing out how the saved are added to the church by God, he says:

> Since this was done each day as they were saved—the same day they were saved—it follows that no saved persons ever remained out of the church overnight. The idea, therefore, of being a saved

---

9. Ibid.
10. Ibid.

person, a Christian, and not being in the church is not only
unscriptural; it is absurd. One could no more be saved and not be
added to the church than one could be born and not thereby be
added to the family into which one is born.[11]

To erase any doubt of what Brewer meant, notice what he said—
after the first part of Foster's citation—on pages 165–66:

We become children of God, and, therefore, members of the church
of God by the spiritual birth—the birth of water and the Spirit—or
by conversion or by obeying the gospel. Nothing less than this can
make anyone a Christian—a member of the church in the true
sense.[12]

Does this sound like Brewer believed there are children of God in
a right relationship in the denominations? Ah, but there is more.

THE REST OF BREWER'S LECTURE

The last sentence in Foster's citation is taken from the section in
Brewer's lecture titled "Sectarianizing Scriptural Phraseology." The
sentence is in the middle of a lengthy paragraph on pages 175–76.
Read the following and judge how fair Foster's quotation of Brewer
is:

The people who started out to restore the New Testament church
and who adopted the maxims, "Where the Bible speaks, we speak;
where the Bible is silent, we are silent" and "Bible names for Bible
things, and Bible thoughts in Bible terms" have fallen into the error
of using Bible terms in a sectarian sense. When we used Bible
designations in their proper sense, we could, with no amount of
persuasion, induce our friends among the sects to apply these terms
to us. They would concede that we were Christians but they vehe-
mently insisted that we were "Campbellites"—that is, that we belonged to a sect of Christians. Our fundamental proposition was to
destroy all sects and induce all followers of Christ to be Christians
only and this was the one point that brought the bitterest opposition
from all sectarians. They would allow us to differ from them on any
special point of doctrine and still be friendly with us, but they could

---

11. G. C. Brewer, "The New Testament Church and Sectarianism," in *The 1952
    Harding Lectures* (Searcy, AR: Harding, 1952), 164.
12. Ibid., 165–66.

never endure the idea that we were not a sect in the same way that they are sects. They might even concede that we had more truth than any of them had if only we would agree to make our portion of truth the creed of a sect. They did not care what we contended for if only we would make the contention as a sect. That is why our opposition has grown so weak in these days. We have, in spite of ourselves, become a sect whose special purpose is to contend against sectarianism. The word *Campbellite* has about disappeared from the vocabulary of our neighbors. Why? Because they are for us to have a scriptural name if we will give it sectarian limitations. They are ready to concede us the right to form a sect and then to name that sect whatever we choose. They scruple not nor hesitate to cal us "Disciples of Christ" using the capital "D" for disciples and thus making a proper name out of the expression. That denotes a sect and all sectdom is ready to felicitate the newcomer. On the terms "Christian Church" and "Church of Christ" using the capital "c" for church in each case are thus made proper names and are entirely acceptable to our opponents. They have become the name of a sect. They designate a special band of professed Christians and that is all any sect is.[13]

Again, remember what Foster said before the citation: "Doctrinally conservative and loyal to Churches of Christ, these voices have insisted that the bounds of God's family are not confined to our fellowship."[14] He further said, "People like G. C. Brewer (d. 1956) and Monroe Hawley have insisted that we cannot and must not equate our visible fellowship of Churches of Christ, as great and noble as it is, with the universal church."[15] Foster is obviously attributing beliefs to Brewer that Brewer never had.

Brother Brewer wrote a book titled *As Touching Those Who Were Once Enlightened.* This was a response to two men, Reedy and Etter, who had left the church, gone into denominationalism, and had written reasons for leaving. Notice some excerpts from Brewer's booklet:

That one fallacy upon which Reedy and Etter launched their attack is the assumption that the church to which they belonged and from which they were departing is a sect whose doctrines and

13. Ibid., 175–76.
14. Foster, 48–49.
15. Ibid.

practices they had ceased to believe and to whose arbitrary authority they could no longer submit.

If their assumption were correct—if there is a sect called Church of Christ and if their allegations against it are true and correct, then (1) they did right in leaving that "fellowship" in which, according to their statements, they were not "fellowshipped" in any way, and (2) those of us who belong to the New Testament church have nothing at all to do with this discussion and disaffection. We are no more concerned about denominational disputes in the Church of Christ than we are about disputes over doctrines and practices in any other denomination . . .

No one has ever yet been able to meet the issue on the plea for the return to the New Testament—a restoration of the New Testament church. All have to admit that there was a church in the New Testament and that men were members of it and worked through it to the glory of God without any of the organizations or institutions that we now have. Then why may we not be members of that body and why may we not work and worship now just as New Testament Christians did? Why belong to any church or body that conversion/obedience to the gospel—does not add you to or align you with? Why recognize any head but Christ? (Ephesians 1:20–22; 5:22; Colossians 1:18). Why submit to any authority except the authority of the Lord? Why wear any denominational name or vow allegiance to any denominational authority?[16]

REWRITE HISTORY? STOP!

"He being dead, yet speaketh." It is high time for brethren to raise their voices in opposition to attempts to revise the history of the church of our Lord and insist on a true account. Some of the Bible faculty at Abilene Christian University, Foster in particular, seem determined to affect a transformation of the Lord's church into a denomination—by any means necessary. However, to quote from the *The Who,* "We won't get fooled again!"

All too often we use the terms *Restoration Movement* and *Restoration Plea* without explanation, assuming that everyone understands what the terms mean. However, that assumption can

---

16. Brewer, *As Touching Those Who Were Once Enlightened,* 73–74.

no longer be made. There have been many attempts in recent years to rewrite Restoration history (One such example: using the term *Stone-Campbell Movement* instead of *Restoration Movement*—a subtle attempt to cast churches of Christ in a denominational context, with Barton W. Stone and Alexander Campbell as the founders.) Another is the trend, as we have seen, to use the words *sectarian* and *sectarianism* to describe those who hold true to the New Testament. Until the late twentieth century, those words referred to denominationalism.

What Lard expressed was simply a summation of 1 Peter 4:11: "If any man speak, let him speak as the oracles of God." How can one say what God has said on any matter without going back to the Word of God? When one accepts any part of Scripture as an authoritative rule of faith and practice, he has accepted the Restoration Principle—returning to the Bible for all religious matters—regardless of how little he accepts.

In the long ago, the prophet Jeremiah wrote, "Thus saith the Lord; Cursed be the man that trusteth in man, and maketh flesh his arm, and whose heart departeth from the Lord" (Jeremiah 17:5). This verse summarizes the desire of many of our day—to turn away from what the will of the Lord requires. The Restoration Plea calls for all people to return to the Lord's way in everything religious: "Thus saith the Lord, Stand ye in the ways, and see, and ask for the old paths, where is the good way, and walk therein, and ye shall find rest for your souls" (Jeremiah 6:16). This is what the great pioneer preachers of yesteryear proclaimed. This is what we must proclaim, for it is what the New Testament declares.

OVERLOOKED RESTORATION HISTORY

All too often, when one thinks of the Restoration, he limits his thinking to the nineteenth century and to Alexander Campbell and Barton W. Stone. At least, that is what many in academia seem to do. However, there is ample evidence that the Lord's church was in existence in America—and even Scotland—before Campbell and Stone; indeed, before Thomas Campbell, Alexander Campbell's father, was born.

Near Bridgeport, Alabama, there stands the meeting house of the Rocky Springs Church of Christ. This congregation, which still exists, began in 1803, making it the oldest church of Christ in Alabama.

Thomas Campbell did not come to America until 1807. In 1803 Barton W. Stone had not yet fully broken with Presbyterianism.

But there is more. Near McMinnville, Tennessee, the meeting house of the Old Philadelphia Church of Christ is located, although the congregation has not been in existence for many years. The earliest documented date for the congregation is approximately the same as that of Rocky Springs, although there is adequate evidence to suggest the congregation was meeting as early as 1798. Further, the Rock Springs Church of Christ, near Celina, Tennessee—which is still in existence—began in 1805. Thus, there are several historic places indicating the Restoration predates Campbell and Stone.

In Britain there is ample evidence that congregations existed long before Campbell and Stone. One such example should be sufficient. There exists a record of a church of Christ near London that dates back to the seventeenth century. It states (all spelling as it appears in the original):

> This booke is for the use off that Church of Christ in Broughton Ffurnessfells and Cartmel whereof Mr. Gabrill Camelford is teaching elder. 18th day of the sixth month called August 1669. A Church of Christ was founded in order and faith drawn together in the fellowship and order of the Gospel of Jesus Christ. All the house of William Rawlinge off Tottlebank in Doulton in Furness there weare present, and assisted Mr. George Lurkham pastor off a Church of Christ in Cumberland and Mr. Roger Sawrey of Broughton Tower, a member of Christ and off that particular Church in London of which Mr. George Coackine is teachinge elder.[17]

Later in the document, this amazing statement is recorded:

> The 10th day of the 11th month called January 1693 the church being solomnly gathered together at Broughton Tower after prayer and the word preached called Mr. Roger Sawrey, Mr. David Crossley, William Braithwhaite and William Robinson to office of elders in the church.[18]

Amazing, is it not, that here we have a group of people, long before Campbell and Stone, attempting to follow the ancient order?

---

17. http://www.christianhomesite.com/belfast/text/records.htm.
18. Ibid.

Those people—both within and without the Lord's church—who attempt to wed us to Campbell and Stone must seriously rethink their efforts. The fact is, there have been many efforts over many centuries to restore the ancient order of the New Testament. While they were not flawless in their obedience, they are to be commended for their efforts. May we all strive to manifest the same spirit in our endeavors. For true restoration to take place, we must go back—not to Rome, not to Constantinople, not to Mecca, but to Jerusalem! We can, and we must, be about the business of restoring pure New Testament Christianity in the twenty-first century.

QUESTIONS FOR DISCUSSION

1. Discuss the similarities between Leftist revisionists concerning communism, and Leftist revisionists in the church.

2. Considering what he did to a quote from G. C. Brewer, what does it say about the credibility of Douglas Foster as a historian?

3. Did Brewer advocate fellowship with the denominations? How do you know?

4. What early congregations do you know about that predate Campbell and Stone?

CHAPTER NINE

The Jesus Seminar

On June 26, 2000, the ABC television network produced a documentary that was nothing short of audacious. Entitled, "Peter Jennings Reports: The Search for Jesus," it purported to be an unbiased account of the anchorman's "search" for Jesus via academic scholars and trips to Palestine. However, what resulted was a showcase for the most liberal views imaginable—namely, those of the Jesus Seminar.

As is the case usually, television was far behind the loop. Actually, the views that were aired have been simmering for the past fifteen years, ever since the Jesus Seminar began. In 1985, Robert W. Funk, Marcus Borg, and John Dominic Crossan launched the seminar as a way of jump starting the so-called "quest for the historical Jesus," which refers to three previous liberal attempts to divorce the man Jesus from the divine Son of God.

The first quest, dating back to the seventeenth century and lasting into the eighteenth, incorporated hardheaded rationalism, Hegelianism ("which views reason as not merely the arbiter of what is real, but also of reality itself"),[1] and old-fashioned liberalism concerning the supernatural and the nature of Jesus.

Albert Schweitzer, who won the Nobel Peace Prize in 1952 for his work in Africa, penned *The Quest of the Historical Jesus* in 1906. In it he not only was critical of previous attempts to discover the "real" Jesus, but he also went much further. Consider what he says concerning the death of Jesus:

> There is silence all around. The Baptist appears, and cries: "Repent, for the Kingdom of Heaven is at hand." Soon after that comes Jesus,

---

1. Robert B. Strimple, *The Modern Search for the Historical Jesus* (Philipsburg, New Jersey, 1995), 25.

and in the knowledge that He is the coming Son of Man lays hold of the wheel of the world to set it moving on that last revolution which is to bring all ordinary history to a close. It refuses to turn, and He throws Himself upon it. Then it does turn; and crushes Him. Instead of bringing in the eschatological conditions, He has destroyed them. The wheel rolls onward, and the mangled body of the one immeasurably great Man, who was strong enough to think of Himself as the spiritual ruler of mankind and to bend history to His purpose, is hanging upon it still. That is His victory and His reign.[2]

One can easily see that Schweitzer's Jesus is not only delusional, but also not a "great Man." Obviously, his view is false. It has also fallen out of favor with most scholars today.

"WE CAN NOW KNOW ALMOST NOTHING"

The second quest developed out of skepticism that developed in the early twentieth century concerning the presuppositions of those involved in the first quest. However, instead of affirming the integrity of the Gospel accounts and the supernatural nature of inspiration, there emerged an even more radical attitude, namely, that one cannot trust the Gospel accounts at all. It was exemplified by the work of Rudolf Bultmann, who summed up his view in one sentence: "I do indeed think that we can now know almost nothing concerning the life and personality of Jesus."[3] According to Bultmann, one must discard the "husk" of "mythology" in the New Testament (namely, the historical), so that the "kernel" of truth *(kerygma)* might remain. Ironically, Bultmann himself was disdainful of any quest into who Jesus was. It took a disciple of his, Ernst Kasemann, to begin the second quest in earnest. Those involved incorporated much of Bultmann's beliefs. His was an existential philosophy, relying heavily upon the just-emerging method of form criticism. The presupposition behind this is that the early church was the primary developer in the origin of Christianity. This view is an article of faith, it seems, among those affiliated with the Jesus Seminar today.

Criticism of Bultmann led to the third quest in the latter half of the twentieth century. Those involved, while not willing to go as far left as others, were nonetheless not accepting the total truth of the

2. Ibid., 84.
3. Ibid., 117.

New Testament. That quest, while still ongoing, has not gained much traction among the elite.

Thus, the Jesus Seminar was begun. Although wishing to distinguish themselves from the earlier quests, one is struck by how the presuppositions are similar. For example, in a debate concerning the work of the seminar, Marcus Borg contributed a chapter entitled "The Irrelevancy of the Empty Tomb."[4] At any rate, Funk, Borg, and Crossan led the movement to reexamine the New Testament evidence concerning Jesus.

THE COLOR-CODED OPINION

The cadre of scholars who followed their lead endeavored to determine what Jesus "really said," as opposed to what they thought was added later by Jesus' followers. The method they employed was farcical. The scholars actually voted on each biblical passage. They did this by casting color-coded beads into a box. Red meant "Jesus undoubtedly said this or something very like it." Pink meant "Jesus probably said something like this." Gray implied "Jesus did not say this, but the ideas contained in it are close to his own." Finally, black meant "Jesus did not say this; it represents the perspective or content of a later and/or different tradition."

The result of such was *The Five Gospels: What Did Jesus Really Say?*, published at the end of 1993. This volume prints all of the passages in the four Gospels, color-coded as per the previous description, plus the apocryphal "Gospel of Thomas." What gained the book so much attention at the time was the proportion of the color code. Less than 20 percent of all the sayings attributed to Jesus was colored either red or pink. Only one verse of Mark was colored red; just fifteen sayings of all the Gospels combined. Seventy-five sayings are colored pink, while 416 are colored gray, and 886 are colored black. Almost all of John is totally rejected, as is the case with all of Jesus' claims about Himself. Yet, this has been represented as "mainstream."

---

4. Paul Copan, ed. *Will The Real Jesus Please Stand Up?* (Grand Rapids: Baker, 1998), 117–28.

There are other reasons to emphatically reject the conclusions of the Jesus Seminar. Its presuppositions are corrupted by liberal ideology. Consider:

- Jesus is not allowed to speak, according to the seminar, in any way except in parables or aphorisms. In other words, Jesus never preached full sermons or engaged in controversy.

- Jesus is also not allowed to address many topics that the Gospels record Him saying. Among those are His Messianic claims, predictive statements, His coming crucifixion, and the Judgment. In addition, He is not allowed to quote Scripture or compare His teachings to the Law of Moses.

- The seminar's Jesus is not thoroughly Jewish, but rather resembles more a Cynic sage, Oriental guru, or Greco-Roman philosopher.

- The seminar's Jesus dies, with little or no explanation why. Strange, is it not, that such an eccentric character as they would have us accept is crucified because He poses a threat to the establishment? John Dominic Crossan even goes so far as to say that Jesus' body was devoured by a pack of wild dogs at the foot of the cross.

- The Jesus Seminar also relies upon the "Gospel of Thomas," which is Gnostic in character and dates back no further than A.D. 400, with a possibility of being written about A.D. 150. However, the Jesus Seminar suggests a date for the document as early as A.D. 50–60, earlier than their dates for the four Gospels.

- The seminar flatly rejects the notion that the Jews had anything to do with Jesus' death; they do this, they contend, to counter anti-Semitism, which they say comes from the Gospel accounts. In their world, Pilate is the chief culprit.

- Above all else, the seminar rejects anything remotely resembling the miraculous. Included in this are the virgin birth, raising people from the dead, and Jesus' own resurrection. Even in the one instance when they do concede the supernatural—Jesus' healings of the people—they claim it is no different from "healings" performed by Eastern mystics and shamans.

DISDAIN OF BIBLICAL EVIDENCE

In 1998, the seminar produced another book, *The Acts of Jesus*. It purported to show what Jesus did and didn't do. But as is the case with their previous work, the sages involved in the project demonstrated disdain for the New Testament evidence. During this "second phase" of the seminar, lasting from 1991 to 1996, they examined 176 events. Again, they utilized the same methodology—voting by casting beads into a box. Of the 176 events, only 29 received either a red or a pink rating—just 16 percent of the total. Only 10 events received a red rating.

What do they have to say for themselves? Consider what Robert W. Funk wrote in the introduction to *The Acts of Jesus:*

> For those who believe the Bible to be the word of God a 16 percent historical accuracy rate may seem ridiculously low. Why did the seminar end up with so many black (largely or entirely fictive) and gray (possible but unreliable) reports? The results should not be surprising to critical scholars—those whose evaluations are not predetermined by theological considerations.[5]

One can detect intellectual snobbery in that quote. As has been shown, the participants in the seminar very definitely had liberal presuppositions. Consider their attitude concerning the Gospels:

> In the absence of hard information, scholars theorize that the New Testament Gospels were comprised during the last quarter of the first century by third-generation authors on the basis of folk memories preserved in stories that had circulated by word of mouth for decades.[6]

Also, they say that the author of Mark "was not an eyewitness."[7] They refer to "the evangelist given the name Matthew"[8] and that Luke "is at least a third-generation Christian scribe."[9] In addition, they assert "Luke's knowledge of events in the larger world is faulty."[10] As if that

---

5. Robert W. Funk and the Jesus Seminar, *The Acts of Jesus* (San Francisco: HarperSan Francisco, 1998), 1.
6. Ibid., 2.
7. Ibid., 4.
8. Ibid.
9. Ibid., 5.
10. Ibid.

were not enough, the assertion is made that much of what is written in the New Testament about what Jesus did is simply folklore. To illustrate what they mean, they refer to the so-called "Roswell Incident," in which a flying saucer was supposed to have crashed in Roswell, New Mexico. The comparison is then made between sorting folklore from truth in that incident, and doing the same in the Gospels.[11] How can anyone reasonably claim to have an unbiased attitude toward the New Testament, with all of these presuppositions in play?

MEDIA SAVVY

Consider something else. On the dust jacket of *The Acts of Jesus,* the conclusions that were reached are listed. Consider some of them:

• Jesus of Nazareth was born in Nazareth, not in Bethlehem.

• Jesus practiced healing without the use of ancient medicine or magic, relieving afflictions we now consider psychosomatic.

• He did not walk on water, feed the multitude with loaves and fishes, change water into wine, or raise Lazarus from the dead.

• The empty tomb is a fiction—Jesus did not rise bodily from the dead.

How can the "scholarship" of the seminar be taken seriously when such erroneous beliefs are fostered on the public? The fact is, it is being taken seriously. One thing that distinguishes the Jesus Seminar is its media-savvy instinct. Not only did ABC produce the special mentioned previously, but also PBS produced a "Frontline" documentary purporting to be about Christianity: "From Jesus to Christ— The First Christians." In it the seminar's views were presented as the authoritative word on the New Testament, without any kind of dissenting voices heard. Not only is that indicative of poor journalism, it also is a perversion of the Word of God. Christianity was presented to have been an evolving religion, originating in large measure from the early followers of Jesus and the "oral tradition" that supposedly fueled the movement. Such is preposterous.

---

11. Ibid., 5–7.

RESPONDING TO THE THREAT

The threat of the Jesus Seminar to the truth can be seen in the flood of books, articles, lectures, and videos that have been produced with its backing. The mere fact that ABC would assign its news department, with its marquee reporter, to cover it, attests to the seriousness of the threat. If one tells a lie often enough and loud enough, some people will eventually believe it. Such is the case with the Jesus Seminar.

This is not the first time people have attacked the credibility of the Gospels and the deity of our Lord. However, we are now living in an advanced technological age. Information is being produced faster and is more accessible than at any time in the history of the world. This means that not only can the truth be proclaimed widely; so can error. The challenge to the Lord's church is deadly serious.

Having said that, there are some observations that must be made. First, not much has been said in print by our brethren about the Jesus Seminar. This must change. The threat is real. Our pens must go to work to educate brethren and equip them to stand firm against any attack on our Lord.

Second, our colleges, universities, and schools of preaching must address the threat of the seminar, if they are not already doing so. Preachers must know how to give an answer to these issues; the day is fast coming when our brethren in this country will have to start from scratch in order to teach the truth.

Third, the situation is looking more and more like the situation that existed at the turn of the previous century. That is, "destructive criticism" invaded our schools and pulpits. John William McGarvey fought against it, as well as Hall Laurie Calhoun. But in the final analysis, liberal theology gained the upper hand as the twentieth century dawned. Can we say the same is true today?

SOUL-SEARCHING QUESTIONS

Let us pursue this matter further. Our brethren on the Left deem themselves to be the most scholarly among us. They also present themselves to be the most spiritual, understanding better than anyone the person of Jesus and His sacrifice. But why are they silent concerning the Jesus Seminar? Surely they above anyone would respond quickly and firmly to it. Could it be that the Left quietly holds to at least some of the same views as the seminar? Is this why Pepperdine, Abilene, and Lipscomb have been silent with respect to Funk, Borg, and Crossan? We have already seen the public spectacle of one belittling the virgin birth. As we have seen, Carroll Osburn in *The Peaceable Kingdom* has put forth a view of inspiration, which is neo-orthodox, at best. Could those be the precursors to open attacks on the inspiration of the Bible? Only time will tell.

Critical scholarship must also be re-examined in light of the seminar. That is, trust in the methods of such must be limited. Is it not significant that the seminar is simply taking the liberal solution concerning the "Synoptic Problem" to its logical end?

Modern critical scholarship has been accepted by many in religion. Even within the body of Christ, many facets of critical scholarship have been incorporated without question—including the matter of the inspiration of the Gospels. However, not everyone has unquestioningly submitted to modern criticism. The late Rex A. Turner, Sr. taught a class at Southern Christian University, now Regions University, entitled, "The Synoptic Gospels." In the class notes, notice what he says concerning the views of too many today:

> In the hands of liberals, however, the study of the Synoptic Gospels is not nearly so innocent.
>
> - The liberals come with the doctrine of the priority of Mark.
> - That the Gospel of Mark was written earlier than the Gospels of Matthew and Luke.
> - That Mark copied from a source which the liberals label, Marcus Q.
> - That the Gospels of Matthew and Luke were copied from Mark, together with the compilation of other sources.
> - That Matthew and Luke were completed in the second half of the first century.
>
> Now, assuming for the moment that the liberals are correct in their holdings, what would this do for your concept of inspiration?[12]

Indeed. Brother Turner forcefully and deliberately taught the truth concerning the Gospels, and in turn asked what he called "Questions That Are Soul Searching":

----

12. Rex A. Turner, Sr. *The Synoptic Gospels: NT 5306* (class notes, undated), 1.

- Was Jesus a mere legend?

- Are the documents of the gospels substantial, or reasonable, beyond doubt, or are they mere legends?

- Is Jesus to be accepted only as a great moral teacher?[13]

Brother Turner answered the first question "no"; the second question, "beyond doubt"; and the third question, "no; He is the Son of God—the Messiah." In addition, he answered the claims of liberals in his book *Systematic Theology*. In his chapter, "The Supposed Priority of the Gospel of Mark," he sets forth the truth of the matter. Brother Turner dates Matthew at A.D. 50, Luke at A.D. 58, Mark at A.D. 67, and John around A.D. 85–95. He also gives the purpose for each Gospel. Matthew wrote of Christ as the "King" for Jewish Christians, Luke wrote of Him as the "Redeemer" for the Gentiles, Mark wrote of Him as the "Servant" for the Romans, and John wrote of Him as the "Word" to supply information not supplied by the other three.[14]

AN ISSUE OF INSPIRATION

In closing the chapter, brother Turner included some remarks which need to be heeded by all of us today:

> The issue at stake is inspiration. Are the Old and New Testaments inspired, or are they the product of mere men? A corollary of the issue of inspiration is the question of whether or not there is an omnipotent, omniscient, omnipresent God—a creator who is perfect in holiness and righteousness? If the Scriptures are not inspired, how can a mere man, be he, by his own admission ever so intelligent and creative, as to account for the theme of the Bible—that is, God, Man, and Jesus the Son of God? Those who spend their lives in efforts to discredit the inspiration of the scriptures are impelled by self-esteem and haughty pride. God has displayed his creative powers. Paul wrote:

> "For the invisible things of him since the creation of the world are clearly seen, being perceived through the things that are made, even his everlasting power and divinity; that they may be without

---

13. Ibid., 7–8.
14. Turner, *Systematic Theology* (Montgomery, AL: Alabama Christian School of Religion, 1990), 42–47.

excuse: because that, knowing God, they glorified him not as God, neither gave thanks; but became vain in their reasonings, and their senseless heart was darkened. Professing themselves to be wise, they became fools, and changed the glory of the incorruptible God for the likeness of an image of corruptible man, and of birds, and four-footed beasts, and creeping things. Wherefore God also gave them up in the lusts of their hearts unto uncleanness" (Romans 1:20–24).

The case is that the liberal Old and New Testament scholars stand under Paul's indictment and condemnation.[15]

As he was on so many other matters, Rex Turner Sr. was right on target. His judgment stands the test of time and must be considered by all those who take seriously the claims of modern critical scholarship concerning the Synoptic Gospels.

THE ELUSIVE "Q" DOCUMENT

The centerpiece of the liberals' "solution" to the Synoptic Problem— the so-called "Q" document—is a chimera, a will-o'-the-wisp that exists only in the minds of those willing to accept it as true. Such a document has never been discovered, or has ever been shown even to exist. Surely it is more than a coincidence that the participants in the Jesus Seminar give much space to the "Q" document, and the four-source theory of the Synoptics.[16] This should be enough to give one pause before being willing to accept such as true.

It becomes clear, as well, that the Roman Catholic Church bears a degree of responsibility for bringing on such liberal attacks. Many of the participants in the seminar have Catholic backgrounds, and are reacting against the ritualism of the denomination. However, they have gone into total infidelity.

Simon Greenleaf was Dane Professor of Law at Harvard University from 1833–48. He was also instrumental in organizing the university's law program. His three-volume work, *A Treatise on the Law of Evidence,* is considered a classic of American jurisprudence. In 1874 he authored a book, *The Testimony of the Evangelists.* In it he

---

15. Ibid., 47–48.
16. Funk, Roy W. Hoover, and the Jesus Seminar, *The Five Gospels* (San Francisco: Harper San Francisco, 1993), 12–18.

applied the same rules of evidence he himself authored to the validity of the Gospels. In the course of so doing, he made a statement that is even truer today than it was then:

> But the Christian writer seems, by the usual course of the argument, to have been deprived of the common presumption of charity in his favor; and reversing the ordinary rule of administering justice in human tribunals, his testimony is unjustly presumed to be false, until it is proven to be true. This treatment, moreover, has been applied to them all in a body; and, without due regard to the fact that, being independent historians, writing at different periods, they are entitled to the support of each other: they have been treated, in the argument, almost as if the New Testament were the entire production, at once, of a body of men, conspiring in a joint fabrication, to impose a false religion upon the world. It is time that this injustice should cease; that the testimony of the evangelists should be admitted to be true, until it can be disproved by those who would impugn it; that the silence of one sacred writer on any point should no more detract from his own veracity or that of the other historians, than the like circumstance is permitted to do among profane writers; and that the Four Evangelists should be admitted in corroboration of each other, as readily as Josephus and Tacitus, or Polybius and Livy.[17]

In the final analysis, Peter Jennings, ABC, the Jesus Seminar, and Left-wing scholars do not determine truth. Only God's Word does that. The salient question to consider is simply: Can we trust the Bible, or not? We can, and we must.

---

17. Simon Greenleaf, *The Testimony of the Evangelists* (Grand Rapids: Kregel Classics, 1995), 30.

QUESTIONS FOR DISCUSSION

1. In the final analysis, will God's Word always stand against repeated attacks? (1 Peter 1:23–25).

2. There will ever be those who are "ever learning, and never able to come to the knowledge of the truth" (2 Timothy 3:7). Should we be intimidated by "scholars"?

3. Whenever an elaborate theory is put forth as the basis of understanding the Bible (e.g., the Four-Source Theory and "Q"), should we accept it?

4. Are the four Gospels totally reliable and trustworthy? Defend you answer. Must we submit to them?

CHAPTER TEN

Is Young Absalom Safe—
In His Youth Group?

Young people in churches of Christ are a potential source of much good. Their energy, enthusiasm, and abilities can assist the local congregation in a multitude of ways. When properly led by godly elders, a youth group can accomplish things that could not accomplished otherwise. When a youth minister is sound and conscientious, he can help youth to be all they can become in Christ.

But the reality is, too many youth groups, too many youth ministers, and too many elderships are practicing things contrary to the Word of God. Consequently, youth events are designed to attract as many young people as possible, often by promoting unscriptural innovations and featuring speakers who teach false doctrine.

SOULSTOCK—AN EXAMPLE OF THE PROBLEM

Consider, for example, an event called "Soulstock." Held near Athens, Alabama, Soulstock began in 1998 as a youth rally for a congregation that was the result of a split. Indeed, the group had been marked and withdrawn from by the elders of the West Hobbs Street congregation. Still, Soulstock grew to the point that major CCM recording artists, such as Rebecca St. James and Audio Adrenaline were featured.

On the Soulstock Web site, there is a page entitled "I Want to Be a Christian." Given the fact that the church that began the event was affiliated with churches of Christ, one would think the right answer would be given. Examine the following and judge for yourself:

> If you would like to enter into a relationship with Jesus Christ,
> all you have to do is ask Him through prayer. Read this prayer, and
> see if it expresses the desire of your heart.

"Dear God, I now know that Jesus is Your Son and that He died on the cross and was raised from the dead. Because I have sinned and need forgiveness, I ask Jesus to be my Savior and Lord. I am willing to change the direction of my life by acknowledging Jesus as my Lord and Savior, and by turning away from my sins. Thank you for giving me forgiveness, eternal life, and hope for today and all my tomorrows. In Jesus' name I pray, amen."

Use this prayer if it expresses your feelings, or pray a similar prayer in your own words, committing your life to Jesus and asking Him for His gift of eternal life.[1]

Later on the same page, under the question "What happens after you receive hope from God," there is listed this point: "You will publicly profess your faith by being baptized (Matthew 28:19–20; Luke 3:21; Romans 6:4)."[2]

That this is contradictory to New Testament teaching is quite obvious. God's Word plainly teaches what one must do to be saved, and a "sinner's prayer" is not mentioned. Indeed, the people at Pentecost cried out, "Men and brethren, what shall we do?" (Acts 2:37) Peter replied, "Repent ye, and be baptized, every one of you, in the name of Jesus Christ, for the remission of your sins, and ye shall receive the gift of the Holy Ghost" (Acts 2:38). Jesus clearly stated, "He that believeth and is baptized shall be saved; but he that believeth not shall be damned" (Mark 16:16).

Additionally, on the same Web site there is an interesting statement:

One of the most important concepts that led to the development of Soulstock was unity. As we began to plan for the next youth event, there were several different denominations represented. Our focus was to promote Christ and to promote unity. Not long after we began to meet the next year we created a mission statement.

"To plant the seed of Jesus Christ in the hearts of our youth and to promote a spirit of unity among all who put their trust in Him." That continues to sum up what Soulstock is all about.[3]

---

1. http://www.soulstock.com/.
2. Ibid.
3. Ibid.

POLLUTING WORSHIP

Under the heading of "Church Sponsors," several denominations are listed. Such is typical of too many youth events within churches of Christ. On the Soulstock Web site, over and again the phrase "worship and praise" is used to describe what takes place. The 2001 event was titled "A Worship Odyssey." Subsequent years were given the monikers: "United Worship," "Worship Him in Spirit and Truth," and "Worthy of Worship."[4]

This is all too common at youth events. Worship, in the mind of the organizers, can—and indeed, must—include praise teams. One of the earliest proponents of praise teams within churches of Christ is Keith Lancaster. The founder of the group *Acappella,* Lancaster is also the worship minister at Madison Church of Christ in Nashville. In an interview with *The Christian Chronicle,* Lancaster comments:

> As far as music in worship services, I believe my work with praise teams bolsters the tradition of a cappella, congregational singing and helps carry it into the future. Praise teams assist the worship leader by helping to teach parts, maintaining the pitch and tempo, and encouraging everyone to sing out.[5]

He also comments, "Throughout *Acappella's* history, there have been four primary goals: glorify God, encourage Christians, reach the lost, and provide a godly alternative to worldly music."[6]

Notice that no justification is given from Scripture for incorporating such into worship. Indeed, it is assumed that God will accept it. As we have seen, though, worship that pleases God must be in harmony with His will. Nowhere in the New Testament can one find any indication of praise teams or special music. In *Among the Scholars,* we gave the reasons why special music in worship is wrong. Nevertheless, there are many—too many—who clamor to have it in worship.

Consider the nature of worship. Jesus said, "God is a spirit; and they that worship him must worship him in spirit and in truth" (John 4:24). Worship involves both an attitude and an action. Whatever is

---

4. Ibid.
5. http://sites.silaspartners.com/partner/Article_Display_Page/ 0,,PTID25485 | CHID127205 | CIID1659416,00.html.
6. Ibid.

done in worship—whether in a public assembly or a private gathering —must be done according to the New Testament.

Some claim that anything scriptural and right for one Christian to do in the presence of other Christians is scriptural and right in the presence of all the Christians in any location (i.e., the assembled congregation). This is said in defense of special music, but it assumes that which is to be proved—that is, special music being scriptural. Also the statement mentions nothing about worship, so anything could be incorporated into worship, using this reasoning.

Not only does such take place at youth rallies, but also at colleges and universities affiliated with churches of Christ. Quite often congregations will send their youth groups to events at these institutions, oblivious to the false teachers who are prevalent, and the praise teams that perform.

Consider the "Summer Celebration" (formerly the Summer Lectureship) at David Lipscomb University. The 2005 event featured such speakers as Joe Beam, Jeff Walling, Randy Harris, and John Mark Hicks.[7] That these men are false teachers, there is no doubt. Each evening there was a period of contemporary "praise and worship" led by Ken Young and Hallal, a praise team.[8]

Parents, Elders, Wake Up!

Why are congregations willingly supporting false teaching? Why do parents send their children to be indoctrinated by the liberal Left without any concern? The answers to these questions are diverse but must be considered. Perhaps some parents simply do not know what is going on at youth events. They are so preoccupied with their own lives that they trust youth leaders and believe all is well when their children attend these rallies.

Other parents are fully aware of what is going on. And what's more, they encourage it and even participate in it themselves. Quite often these parents have been active participants in dividing congregations. For them such events are manifestations of the winds of

---

7. Lipscomb Summer Celebration.pdf
8. Ibid.

change blowing through churches of Christ—and they want their children to be part of it.

Still other parents, with some reservations, allow their children to attend such events. They do not want their children to be left out of the youth group, and they possibly do not know themselves how to determine from Scripture whether or not these events are right.

The same reasons apply, to a certain extent, to elderships. Those who allow their youth groups to attend events that are questionable are either uninformed, totally approving, or hesitant to make waves. Complicating the matter is the fact that some elders do not want to lose members. In order to keep a group, they will give in to whatever demand they make. As a result, the congregation becomes vulnerable to radical change in worship—brought in by the youth minister and those of like mind.

SEE YOU AT THE POLE—A CLOSER EXAMINATION

One event that many youth groups support happens at schools across the country. Titled "See You at the Pole," teenagers participate in gathering around the flagpole at their high school for a period of prayer. While this seems to be admirable, a closer examination shows this to be a precursor to more serious problems.

On the Web site for the event, the following history is given:

> A small group of teenagers in Burleson, Texas, came together for a "DiscipleNow" weekend in early 1990. They came seeking God. Little did they know how powerfully God was about to move. On Saturday night God penetrated their hearts like never before. The students were broken before God and burdened for their friends. Compelled to pray, they drove to three different schools that night. Not knowing exactly what to do, they went to the school flagpoles and prayed for their friends, schools, and leaders. Those students had no idea how God would use their obedience.
>
> God used what He did among those teenagers and others who were holding similar prayer meetings at their schools to birth a vision in the hearts of youth leaders across Texas. The vision was that students throughout Texas would follow these examples and meet at their school flagpoles to pray simultaneously. The challenge was named "See You at the Pole" at an early brainstorming session. The vision was shared with 20,000 students in June 1990 at Reunion Arena in Dallas, Texas.

Only God had envisioned how many students would step up to the challenge. At 7:00 A.M. on September 12, 1990, more than 45,000 teenagers met at school flagpoles in four different states to pray before the start of school.

A few months later, a group of youth ministers from all over the country gathered together for a national conference in Colorado. Many of them reported that their students had heard about the prayer movement in Texas and were equally burdened for their schools. No other events had been planned, but it was clear that students across the country would be creating their own national day of student prayer. There was no stopping them.

On September 11, 1991, at 7:00 A.M., one million students gathered at school flagpoles all over the country. From Boston, Massachusetts, to Los Angeles, California, students came together to pray. Some sang, some read Scripture, but most importantly, they prayed. Like those first students, they prayed for their schools, for their friends, for their leaders, and for their country.

As in all great movements of prayer, "See You at the Pole" did not begin in the hearts of people. It began in the heart of God. God used the obedience of a small group of teenagers to ignite what has become an international movement of prayer among young people.

Since 1991, "See You at the Pole" has grown to God-sized proportions. Within only a couple of years, students were praying in several countries around the world. Now, more than 3 million students from all 50 states participate in SYATP. Students in more than 20 countries take part. In places like Canada, Guam, Korea, Japan, Turkey, and the Ivory Coast, students are responding to God and taking seriously the challenge to pray.

God is continuing to call His people to repentance and prayer. Countless inspiring testimonies of how He has used "See You at the Pole" to bring students to Christ and to change lives affirm God's power to answer those who cry out to Him in humble dependence. Bible clubs, weekly prayer meetings, and other ministries have begun on campuses where students participated in SYATP.[9]

On the same Web site, the supporting ministries are listed. Numerous denominations are included, along with denominational organizations. In other words, when one supports this event, he or she is having fellowship with religious groups that are at variance with God's Word. It is not a matter of benign participation in a civic

---

9. http://www.syatp.org/info/history.html.

event; the express purpose is to "bring students to Christ." How can a student be led to Christ if he or she does not learn what Christ requires one to do to be saved?

The SYATP Web site also includes reports of past events. In one such report, the following is stated:

> Many who told their stories on the SYATP website indicated that participants were spiritually responsive. A girl at Westview High School in San Diego, California, led one of her teachers to Christ. Three students of the sixty who attended at Lincoln High School in Stockton, California, "gave their lives to Jesus" at the pole, according to an attendee. A student at Jensen Beach (Florida) High School reported that there were eight hundred who attended a community post-pole rally the evening of September 15. He wrote, "That night about 150 teenagers brought their friends to Christ or recommitted their lives to Christ."[10]

How can young people from churches of Christ effectively present the New Testament truth on salvation when denominational groups are in control? Such would be difficult, at best.

Regardless of those who are departing from the truth, there are still many young people in the Lord's church who want to do what is right. Likewise, there are still preachers and youth leaders who are committed to being active with young people—in the right way. Elderships must be dedicated to shepherding youth groups, as well as all other Christians. In so doing, they will protect them from false teachers and wrong worship practices. They will provide the proper spiritual diet and feed them what is wholesome. Parents will assume responsibility for bringing up their children in the right way. In so doing, one will not have to ask, "Is young Absalom safe?" He will know, and take comfort!

---

10. *See You At The Pole Perspectives* #1, September 17, 2004

Questions for Discussion

1. Does "Soulstock" promote a biblical view of how to become a Christian?

2. Is it right to incorporate special music into worship?

3. Does it matter where our children go to youth rallies?

4. Why is "See You at the Pole" troublesome?

CHAPTER ELEVEN

Do We Have the Right Kind of Love?

Paul had less criticism of the brethren in Philippi than any other congregation, but he urged them to grow in love. In Philippians 1:9 he wrote, "And this I pray, that your love may abound yet more and more." He also wanted them to abound "in knowledge and in all judgment." Paul wished for them an intelligent love. This can be accomplished only by growth in knowledge: "But grow in grace, and in the knowledge of our Lord and Savior Jesus Christ" (2 Peter 3:18). Paul wanted their love to be intelligent so they would be able to discern between things worthy and unworthy of their love. We must be able to do the same.

God's Word tells us what we are not to love: "Love not the world, neither the things that are in the world. If any man love the world, the love of the Father is not in him" (1 John 2:15). By way of contrast, Paul writes, "If ye then be risen with Christ, seek those things which are above, where Christ sitteth on the right hand of God. Set your affections on things above, not on things on the earth" (Colossians 3:1–2). We must be able to discern between worldly things and heavenly things.

The things a person allows judges his character. What a person thinks, he talks about; he indulges in things in which he is interested. While the apostle Paul does not specifically tell us in Philippians 1 what a person should think about, he does say we must "approve things that are excellent" (Philippians 1:10). Our love for heavenly things enables us to approve those things that are excellent. What are some objects of the Christian's love?

THREE OBJECTS OF LOVE

The supreme object of our love is God. Matthew 22:37 says, "Thou shalt love the Lord thy God with all thy heart, and with all thy soul, and with all thy mind." We find it easy to love those who love us; for this reason, we should love God supremely. He gave us our being, supplied our every need, and gave His Son to die on the cross for our sins! We should find it easy to love Him! "We love him, because he first loved us" (1 John 4:19). The test of our love is obedience to His will. "For this is the love of God, that we keep His commandments: and His commandments are not grievous" (1 John 5:3). God's requirements of us are not unreasonable. We get our greatest thrills and highest enjoyment when we do things for someone we love. How much more so with God!

We must also love Jesus. He demands more love than anyone does. He said in Matthew 10:37, "He that loveth father or mother more than me is not worthy of me: and he that loveth son or daughter more than me is not worthy of me." It is inconsistent to say we love Jesus and at the same time refuse to follow His teaching. Christ said, "If ye love me, keep my commandments" (John 14:15)—not part of them, not all of them part of the time, but all of them faithfully and constantly! How interesting that many are touting WWJD—What Would Jesus Do?—while at the same time refusing to do what He has said!

Closely following this is our love for the church. Jesus loved it so much that he gave Himself for it (Ephesians 5:25). We should love it enough to give ourselves in His service. If we love the church, we will accept responsibilities in work and worship. Love will cause one to teach a class, lead a prayer, serve at the Lord's table, and assume any task of which he is capable. If we love the church, we will give our money to assist in carrying the gospel to the world. If we love the church, we won't live in a way to bring reproach upon it; for when we do that, we are also crucifying Jesus afresh! We won't bash the church or persecute those who are faithfully proclaiming the truth.

CHURCH BASHING IS NOT LOVE!

How different this is from those on the Left who profess love for Jesus and His church, but who proceed to harshly criticize it—and in one instance, even indicating the belief that Eastern religions are accepted by God. Leroy Garrett writes,

> Whoever—in whatever nation or circumstance—reverences God (in reference to such knowledge he has of him) and does what is right (according to the light of his conscience) is accepted by God. Such ones may not be in covenant relationship with God, but they are "accepted" by him.
>
> Would this not be true of any Iraqi (Muslim), or Indian (Hindu) or Japanese (Buddhist)? If they honor God in their lives, and do what is right—walking by such light God has given them—they are acceptable to God. It was a staggering truth to Peter with all his exclusiveness. It may be equally staggering to us. This is because our parochialism blinds us to the magnanimity of God.[1]

That statement is shocking enough, but consider what he says next:

> In view of such openness on the part of God, it is not surprising that we would find some of his truth in the great religions of the world beside Christianity. And it is a saying worthy of all acceptation that wherever there is truth it is God's truth. If there is truth in the Koran, it is as much God's truth as truth that is found in the Bible. This is because all truth is of God. And God's truth is God's truth wherever it is found—even when quoted by Satan himself![2]

Do these statements evidence a love for God and Christ? To ask is to answer the question. Consider also the following article by Rubel Shelly:

> Much of the division among Christians is over key events of Christian experience. For example, some churches practice what is called "closed communion." They restrict participation in the Lord's Supper to those most like themselves. They invite to the communion (i.e., fellowship) meal of bread and wine only those who hold membership in their own denomination or only those who have already received baptism or only those who subscribe to certain articles of faith. At certain times and places in Christian history, one had to submit to an examination of his or her faith by a person or panel of church officials prior to a time of communion. Those

---

1. http://www.leroygarrett.org/soldieron/number59.htm.
2. Ibid.

judged worthy to participate were then given a token that would be presented at the communion table.

There is also a great deal of division over baptism. Because of certain New Testament texts about the relationship of baptism to Christ or spiritual rebirth or remission of sins, baptism has typically been associated with membership in the Christian community and/ or salvation. Depending on the mode (i.e., sprinkling, pouring, immersion) involved or one's age (i.e., infant, young child, adult) at baptism, a given believer or group might not honor a person's baptism. She might be excluded from membership in a given church. Or she might be judged to be unsaved.

This sort of thing—identifying a single event or ceremony as the badge of Christian identity and spiritual kinship—is fully consistent with modernity. It provides a formula for including some and excluding others. It draws a clear line between those deemed worthy of acceptance and those to be left out of the community. I'm not at all sure this is how things worked in the earliest days of the church.

In a postmodern world, lines of demarcation are a bit more blurred than they were in the period of modernity. And in its most extreme forms, that blurriness is a bad thing. No action is really good or bad; everything is relative to a culture or circumstance. There is no ultimate distinction between truth and error; you have your truth, and I have mine. In these extreme forms of postmodern relativism, Christianity is neither better nor worse than Islam or Buddhism, agnosticism or atheism. One should remember, however, that moral and epistemological relativism was embraced by modernity as well.

The healthier side of postmodernity's rejection of rigid formulas in favor of blurred lines of distinction is not difficult to see and appreciate. Blacks and whites, rich and poor, scholars and illiterates, citizens and refugees—all can have a seat at the same table of opportunity. There will be less class consciousness. There will be fewer acts of unjust discrimination and intolerance.

Within the context of Christian discussion, I am encouraged rather than frightened by what I have called the "healthier side of postmodernity's rejection of rigid formulas." It could very well move believers in Christ away from institutional models of church to an organic model. Christians might think less about institutional religion and more about the body of Christ, less about denominational distinctions and more about organic ties to one another. If that should happen, we might learn to think, speak, and live more as the church did in its early history than it has of late. If it should happen, we just might be more like Christ's original vision for his church.

In particular, what if—in good biblical and postmodern fashion —we thought of salvation more as a process than an event? What if we understood spiritual transformation as something that takes place over time rather than instantly? What if we used biblical figures of speech like "pilgrimage" and "birth" rather than "church member" and "getting saved"? In other words, what if we retrained ourselves so that we no longer looked to a single event like the sinner's prayer, immersion, or a church vote to validate someone's status as a Christian but to the direction and tone of his life over time? What if we looked for direction rather than perfection in one another's spiritual life?

After all, I've known some people who have been baptized but who use God's name in profane ways or abuse their children or mouth and model racism. Is the event of their baptism enough to offset their way of life? Is church membership sufficient to compensate for moral and spiritual failure? On the other hand, I know people whose baptism is defective on my understanding of the Bible but whose passion for God and uprightness of character left no doubt that they were light-years more spiritual than I am. Should I judge them to be lost? Doubt that God's grace is sufficient to cover any defect in their theology while praising it to offset my pride or selfishness?[3]

Such thinking is totally foreign to the New Testament, which clearly indicates what one must do to be saved and clearly reveals the nature of the church.

THREE MORE OBJECTS OF LOVE

We must also love the truth. In 2 Thessalonians 2:10, Paul said people who do not love the truth will be lost. We must be like the noble Bereans of Acts 17, who checked up on inspired men! If we love the truth, we will accept it regardless of the source, and defend it at all cost (Jude 3). Paul told Titus that the mouths of false teachers must be stopped (Titus 1:9–11). If we love the truth today, we will accept this dictum. We need to be like Stephen who was able to defend

---

3. Rubel Shelly, "Being God's Child: Event or Process?" http://www. rubelshelly.com/content.asp?CID=10400.

the truth against those who attempted to dispute it (Acts 6:9–10). Paul did the same; for three months he "spake boldly . . . disputing and persuading the things concerning the kingdom of God" (Acts 19:8).

How different this is from many within the Lord's church, who refuse to stand for what is right and against what is wrong. In Galatians 2:5 Paul says of false teachers: "To whom we gave place by subjection, no, not for an hour; that the truth of the gospel might continue with you." Some elderships today say, "Let them talk." Some of our schools even give them tenured positions and prominent places on lectureships, all in the name of academic freedom.

We also must love one another. "Let brotherly love continue" (Hebrews 13:1). "Seeing ye have purified your souls in obeying the truth through the Spirit unto unfeigned love of the brethren, see that ye love one another with a pure heart fervently" (1 Peter 1:22). Everyone has faults, and sometimes brethren have faults of which we do not approve. However, we must love them in spite of their faults. If God had refused to love us until we were worthy, we would yet be without hope. We need to love the brethren, regardless of what they may say or do. When Jesus died on the cross, He prayed for those who crucified Him! Praying for people will cause us to love them more.

Those on the Left have not truly demonstrated their love for brethren; in dividing congregations, they demonstrate a blatant disregard for the sensibilities of brothers and sisters in Christ. They have forgotten what God says in Proverbs 6:16–19:

> These six things doth the Lord hate: yea, seven are an abomination unto him: a proud look, a lying tongue, and hands that shed innocent blood, an heart that deviseth wicked imaginations, feet that be swift in running to mischief, a false witness that speaketh lies, and he that soweth discord among brethren.

Then we must love the lost. God's love for the lost sent His Son into the world. The love of Christ for the lost made Him willing to die for us. The only way we can show our appreciation for this love is by being involved in some way in assisting the spreading of the gospel. If I love the lost, and have the ability to preach, I need to preach the gospel. If I love the lost, yet cannot preach, I need to give of my means to help send preachers overseas and support my local preacher. If I love the lost, I will take every opportunity to invite them to come hear the gospel preached. Too many members of the church are not willing to love the lost even to this extent. This is one of the reasons the church is not growing as it once did! Paul's love for the lost caused him to "have great heaviness and continual sorrow" (Romans 9:2). Do we? His love for the lost made Him willing to suffer all things (2 Timothy 2:10). We should be just as willing.

TRAITS OF TRUE LOVE

Truly, love is the "more excellent way" (1 Corinthians 12:31). In 1 Corinthians 13:4–7 Paul describes what one does who has love. In verse 4 he says love "suffereth long." That is, because he loves people, the child of God will suffer their insults and injuries a long time. He does not have a "hair trigger." In the same verse, Paul adds, "and is kind." This indicates the child of God is good-natured; tender, not hard-hearted. Also in verse 4, Paul adds "envieth not." Envy is a malicious grudge, which is distressed over the successes of others. True love gives no quarter to such. Then in verse 4, Paul says that love "vaunteth not itself, is not puffed up." That is, the child of God is not full of pride and conceit. In Romans 12:3 Paul wrote, "For I say, through the grace given unto me, to every man that is among you, not to think of himself more highly than he ought to think; but to think soberly, according as God hath dealt to every man the measure of faith."

First Corinthians 13:5 adds several traits to the child of God who possesses true love.

- "Doth not behave itself unseemly." The child of God respects the feelings and wishes of others. His conduct is fitting and appropriate.
- "Seeketh not her own." That is, one's own wealth and pleasure at the expense of others. He seeks good for all people.
- "Not easily provoked." He does not give way to fits of anger; he is calm and patient.
- "Thinketh no evil." Other versions render the phrase, "Taketh no account of evil." Contrary to the trend of today, the child of God does not chalk up insults with a view toward revenge.

Two statements in verse 6 give a stark contrast. "Rejoiceth not in iniquity." The child of God does not rejoice over injustice to anyone— not even one's enemies! "Rejoiceth in the truth." That is, when the truth is taught and practiced. The Christian is to take joy in God's Word being followed.

Verse 7 lists four character traits that ought to describe all Christians.

- "Beareth all things." In spite of wrongs and mistreatments, the child of God does not quit. He keeps on going.

- "Believeth all things." He believes all that is true about people, not just the bad.

- "Hopeth all things." The child of God hopes for the best; he believes in people. He expects good things to come.

- "Endureth all things." Whatever comes—whether it is evils, reversals, trials, betrayals, or losses—he endures.

Focusing our love on the right objects will not only help us grow; it will also help the church to grow. Do you love the Lord? Then show it by how you live each day of your life.

QUESTIONS FOR DISCUSSION

1. What kind of love must the Christian possess?

2. What should be the objects of our love?

3. Examine the statements of Garrett and Shelly. Are these men correct?

4. Why is 1 Corinthians 13 so important?

CHAPTER TWELVE

The Church Needs to Watch

The word *watch* carries with it several meanings. One is, "to be or keep awake." Another suggests, "to keep guard." An additional definition says, "to be on the lookout." When one applies such meanings to the Lord's church, he sees the significance of the word itself.

God wants His church to be awake, always on guard against evils that might creep in to hinder its progress and destroy the peace and harmony for which Jesus prayed. In addition, the church must look ahead for danger signals in order to steer clear of the snares of Satan.

The New Testament is replete with passages suggesting that it is important for Christians to watch. Jesus said, "Watch and pray that ye enter not into temptations" (Matthew 26:41). Paul told Timothy, "Watch thou in all things" (2 Timothy 4:5). Revelation 16:15 says, "Behold, I come as a thief. Blessed is he that watcheth and keepeth his garments, lest he walk naked and they see his shame."

What are we to watch? There are many things that bear watching if we are to be as God would have us be and make the church the kind of church that God wants.

WATCH YOURSELF

First, we must watch ourselves. Occasionally, people will say, "You had better watch that fellow," or, "He (or she) bears watching." However, we need to bear a little watching, too! In Acts 20:28 Paul told the Ephesian elders, "Take heed unto yourselves, and to all the flock, over the which the Holy Ghost hath made you overseers, to feed the church of God which he hath purchased with his own blood." Notice that Paul said first, "Take heed unto yourselves." Some within the body of Christ apparently think that only elders and preachers are to be engaged in looking after the souls of others. It must be remembered, though, that each of us has a soul to look after. We will give an account on the day of judgment for the things we have done; we will either be saved or lost. Thus, we must take heed unto ourselves.

In watching ourselves, we must watch our everyday life. We must see to it that our lives are in harmony with that which we believe and teach. It needs to be such that would grace and adorn the gospel of Christ. Paul told Timothy, "Be thou an example of the believers" (1 Timothy 4:12). His admonition applies to all Christians, not just those who are younger. Our postmodern world normally judges us by how we live, and not necessarily by what we believe and teach. A church member who curses, drinks, and gambles is not a good example of the believers! We must watch ourselves and shun the very appearance of evil in our everyday lives.

In Titus 2:14, Paul said that Christ "gave himself for us, that he might redeem us from all iniquity, and purify unto himself a peculiar people, zealous of good works." Since we are redeemed, we are to be unlike the world. Paul again encourages us in Romans 12:2: "And be not conformed to this world: but be ye transformed by the renewing of your mind, that ye may prove what is that good, and acceptable, and perfect will of God."

THREE "W's" THAT NEED TO BE WATCHED

Each letter of the word *watch* stands for at least three areas that bear watching. Consider the letter "w." We must watch our worship. We must always remember that God is to be pleased above all. In John 4:24, Jesus said, "God is a spirit: and they that worship him must worship him in spirit and in truth." God is the object of our worship, not idols. A few years ago, a Hindu temple opened in Birmingham, Alabama. It received extensive media attention, especially in print. Pictures showed the caretaker "feeding" an idol! Is it not amazing, that in the twenty-first century, people would still worship statues? Paul, in Acts 17, makes it clear that God is to be worshiped.

We "must" worship God. Worship is not an option! We cannot treat times of worship in a cavalier fashion. God deserves our time and devotion. Further, we must worship Him "in spirit," that is, with the right attitude of heart. Our worship must be completely dedicated to

God, and our minds clear of any distractions. Our hearts must be filled with love and gratitude.

We must worship God "in truth." That means, of course, that we must worship as the Bible teaches and not deviate from the instructions given within. Otherwise, our worship is vain. In Matthew 15:9 Jesus said, "But in vain they do worship me, teaching for doctrines the commandments of men." Second John 9–11 warns,

> Whosoever transgresseth, and abideth not in the doctrine of Christ, hath not God. He that abideth in the doctrine of Christ, he hath both the Father and the Son. If there come any unto you, and bring not this doctrine, receive him not into your house, neither bid him God speed: for he that biddeth him God speed is partaker of his evil deeds.

It is clear that any additions, substitutions, and changes in God's plan are wrong. That is why instrumental music, "special music," and other innovations cannot be allowed in worship. Elders must especially be on the lookout for any deviations from the New Testament pattern. Preachers need to proclaim the whole counsel of God concerning these matters.

Then, we must watch our walk. The child of God must walk according to divine directions. In Jeremiah 10:23, the prophet declares, "O Lord, I know that the way of man is not in himself: it is not in man that walketh to direct his steps." Man cannot direct his own life, contrary to what humanistic psychiatry teaches. Paul tells us, "For we walk by faith, not by sight" (2 Corinthians 5:7). And again, "So then faith cometh by hearing, and hearing by the word of God" (Romans 10:17). Our Christian walk must be guided by the Bible. Romans 8:13 warns, "For if ye live after the flesh, ye shall die: but if ye through the Spirit do mortify the deeds of the body, ye shall live." Psalms 119:105 further says, "Thy word is a lamp unto my feet, and a light unto my path."

We must further watch our work. Children of God must be active; always working for the Lord. James asks a rhetorical question: "What doth it profit, my brethren, though a man say he hath faith, and have not works? can faith save him?" (James 2:14). He then declares in verse 24, "Ye see then how that by works a man is justified, and not by faith only." Paul exhorts, "Therefore, my beloved brethren, be ye stedfast, unmoveable, always abounding in the work of the Lord, forasmuch as ye know that your labour is not in vain in the Lord" (1 Corinthians 15:58).

THREE "A's" OF WATCH

The letter "a" also stands for several things we need to watch. Our actions bear watching. How we treat one another is of great importance. Ephesians 4:32 urges, "And be ye kind one to another, tenderhearted, forgiving one another, even as God for Christ's sake hath forgiven you." Peter writes, "Finally, be ye all of one mind, having compassion one of another, love as brethren, be pitiful, be courteous" (1 Peter 3:8). Jesus teaches: "Let your light so shine before men, that they may see your good works, and glorify your Father which is in heaven" (Matthew 5:16).

The appetite of a child of God needs to be watched. No, not physical appetite, rather, what we allow into our souls. Our advanced technological age makes it much easier to fall into temptation and to feed an appetite for sin. It is so important for the child of God to allow the right things to enter his life. Jesus says, "It is written, Man shall not live by bread alone, but by every word that proceedeth out of the mouth of God" (Matthew 4:4). Paul writes, "Whether therefore ye eat, or drink, or whatsoever ye do, do all to the glory of God" (1 Corinthians 10:31). What we desire reflects who we are—as individuals and as congregations.

Then our adversary must be watched. Peter warns, "Be sober, be vigilant; because your adversary the devil, as a roaring lion, walketh about, seeking whom he may devour" (1 Peter 5:8). Peter, of all people, could speak from experience. We need to heed his warning! Jesus' warning to Peter in is chilling:

> And the Lord said, Simon, Simon, behold, Satan hath desired to have you, that he may sift you as wheat: but I have prayed for thee, that thy faith fail not: and when thou art converted, strengthen thy brethren. And he said unto him, Lord, I am ready to go with thee, both into prison, and to death. And he said, I tell thee, Peter, the cock shall not crow this day, before that thou shalt thrice deny that thou knowest me (Luke 22:31–34).

So when Peter warns us about Satan, it resonates. Satan used everything in his power to tempt Peter to commit sin. Today Satan does the same thing to us. Consider Peter's words: "Whom resist stedfast in the faith, knowing that the same afflictions are accomplished in your brethren that are in the world" (1 Peter 5:9). What encouragement! We can overcome the adversary!

"T" UNDER SCRUTINY

The letter "t" in the word "watch" also represents some areas that we need to scrutinize. The child of God must watch his time. Youth especially need to pay attention. Ecclesiastes 12:1 teaches, "Remember now thy Creator in the days of thy youth, while the evil days come not, nor the years draw nigh, when thou shalt say, I have no pleasure in them." Paul exhorts all God's children: "Redeeming the time, because the days are evil" (Ephesians 5:16). Let us resolve to use our time wisely!

Another thing that bears watching is our talents. God has blessed each of us with an ability to do something in His service. The Lord has also given us all something to do along with that ability. If we fail to develop our talents, are we being faithful servants? The one-talent man in Matthew 25 was an honest man. He did not steal his lord's money. As a matter of fact, he took good care of it and did not lie about it. He even brought it back and gave it to him. He could have reasoned, "Since my lord has entrusted me with only one talent, I am insignificant. There's nothing worthwhile that I can do. My lord is a hard man anyway. I will bury the talent."

No doubt, we have people in the church just like that. "I don't have the ability to sing like brother so-and-so." Or, "I don't have the ability to teach like sister so-and-so." Therefore, they reason, there is no need even to try. Brethren, God is a just and merciful God, and He expects us to do only that which He has given us the ability to do! While the parable is not particularly addressing the abilities that children of God possess, it is good for all of us to examine what we are doing in the Lord's service. Of course, not every man can lead singing or read Scripture or teach a class. Not every lady can teach children or other ladies. However, each of us can do something. It may be that your talent is to encourage people to come to church or to be more faithful. It may be your ability to make cards for those who are sick and shut-in. You may be able to prepare meals for those who need them. It matters not how insignificant, God has blessed us in some way. We also need to develop the abilities God has given us. Who knows? It may be that your ability is just waiting to be used!

Then, our tongues need to be watched. Proverbs 15:1 declares, "A soft answer turneth away wrath: but grievous words stir up anger." How needed is this admonition by so many congregations! Much turmoil could be avoided if this were heeded. James 1:26 indicates, "If any man among you seem to be religious, and bridleth not his tongue, but deceiveth his own heart, this man's religion is vain." Let us be careful what we say and how we say it.

Watch Your "C's"

The letter "c" also stands for some areas we need to watch. Our character bears watching. Character is the totality of thoughts, purposes, and deeds of an individual. Are we the same in private as we are in public? Do we easily succumb to Satan's temptations? Do we live our faith, as well as profess it? These questions must be asked— of individuals and congregations.

Our company must be watched. Paul exhorts, "Be not deceived: evil communications corrupt good manners" (1 Corinthians 15:33). Other versions read, "Evil companionships corrupt good morals." How true! Romans 12:2 declares, "And be not conformed to this world: but be ye transformed by the renewing of your mind, that ye may prove what is that good, and acceptable, and perfect, will of God." Don't let the world fit you into its mold.

Then, our conscience must be watched. Paul writes of some who would trouble the church: "Speaking lies in hypocrisy; having their conscience seared with a hot iron" (1 Timothy 4:2). In Acts 24:16 he gives insight into his own practice: "And herein do I exercise myself, to have always a conscience void of offence toward God, and toward men." It takes effort to have a clear conscience, but the reward is worth every effort we make.

EXAMINING THE "H"

Finally, the letter "h" in *watch* represents some areas to examine. All of us should watch our hearts and keep them clean. Satan tries everything to make the hearts of the children of God impure. Pornography is rampant in our society, and the Internet makes it immediately accessible. Greed and covetousness are celebrated in game shows on television and violence is glorified. Solomon warns, "Keep thy heart with all diligence; for out of it are the issues of life" (Proverbs 4:23). In the Sermon on the Mount. Jesus declares, "Blessed are the pure in heart: for they shall see God" (Matthew 5:8). But before one can keep his heart pure and clean, it must be made clean. Peter writes that one's heart is made pure through obedience: "Seeing ye have purified your souls in obeying the truth through the Spirit unto unfeigned love of the brethren, see that ye love one another with a pure heart fervently" (1 Peter 1:22). When one obeys the gospel of Christ, his heart is purified. As we walk in the light, the blood of Jesus continues to cleanse us (1 John 1:7–9).

Our hearing must be watched. Hebrews 2:1 warns, "Therefore we ought to give the more earnest heed to the things which we have heard, lest at any time we should let them slip." Jesus exhorts, "Take heed therefore how ye hear" (Luke 8:18). Then James says:

> But be ye doers of the word, and not hearers only, deceiving your own selves. For if any be a hearer of the word, and not a doer, he is like unto a man beholding his natural face in a glass: for he beholdeth himself, and goeth his way, and straightway forgetteth what manner of man he was. But whoso looketh into the perfect law of liberty, and continueth therein, he being not a forgetful hearer, but a doer of the work, this man shall be blessed in his deed (James 1:22–25).

The child of God, and the Lord's church in general, must watch our heavenly home. Joshua uttered a bold statement that ought to guide all people seeking to be faithful.

> And if it seem evil unto you to serve the Lord, choose you this day whom ye will serve; whether the gods which your fathers served that were on the other side of the flood, or the gods of the Amorites, in whose land ye dwell: but as for me and my house, we will serve the Lord (Joshua 24:15).

The church must always be watching. Are you, as a Christian, helping to that end? Or are you a hindrance? These are questions that beg to be answered. May all of us strive to do the Lord's will in order that the church can be the kind of church that God wants.

QUESTIONS FOR DISCUSSION

1. How do the definitions of *watch* apply to the Lord's church?

2. List some things not in the chapter that the child of God must watch.

3. Is the church in your area watching as it should? Give reasons for your answer.

CHAPTER THIRTEEN

Some Reasons for Hope

It is easy to become discouraged at reports of apostasy among the Lord's people. The temptation to believe that the New Left has the upper hand throughout the brotherhood is ever present. However, developments over the past few years should give us some reasons for hope.

In the January 28, 2001, Twickenham Church of Christ bulletin (Huntsville, Alabama), the elders released a statement by the Nashville Jubilee Board. In it they announced, "For a number of reasons, the Jubilee board has determined that the time has come to put Jubilee to bed." The bulletin article then states, "As a result of rising costs and debt accumulated, the board has decided to officially end Jubilee."[1] Considering the discord Jubilee brought, this came as a breath of fresh air. Yes, there are other Left-oriented gatherings that are still taking place, but Jubilee was the marquee event. Since 1989 the Nashville Jubilee served as the premier gathering east of the Mississippi River for those on the Left.

The Jubilee had an auspicious beginning. The elders in charge invited Jane McWhorter to participate. Jane had spoken at many ladies' days across the country and written many wonderful books for ladies' classes. (She and her husband Don are still faithful in the Lord's work.) During Jane's first class at Jubilee, six or seven men entered the room. She—or some other woman—explained that hers was a class for ladies only. The men left. However, after Jane began to speak, another man entered the room. Jane stopped her lecture and explained gently and tactfully her convictions. The man left. Next day at Jane's request, a guard was posted at the door. Several men sought entrance and were turned away. Jane knew immediately

---

1. Twickenham Church of Christ Bulletin, Jan. 28, 2001.

something was wrong. She informed Don, who was not at Jubilee. Don's attempts to rectify the matter proved futile. He later informed the brotherhood of what was happening in Nashville. Over the next several years, Jubilee continued to get worse.

Year after year, Nashville witnessed a plethora of false teachers coming into the city to espouse their doctrines. Eventually, brethren began to withdraw their support—financially and otherwise. The Jubilee collapsed. No doubt, as a result of the Jubilee debacle there were disillusioned professors and preachers in Nashville, Memphis, Abilene, and Malibu.

SOME PROMISING SIGNS

Consider some other promising signs. *The Christian Chronicle* has never been a bastion of sound biblical teaching, to say the least. However, in the February 2001 issue there appeared a center spread detailing a survey done among 300 congregations. Abilene Christian University provided matching funds for the study, which was part of the "Faith Communities Today (FaCT)," a comprehensive study of American churches. The results of the study were perhaps not what the project leaders expected.

An overwhelming majority of the 300 congregations (86.2 percent) have a single Sunday morning worship service. Of those who have two or more services (13.4 percent), most report the two services are very similar in style (80.6 percent). Only 9.7 percent of those who have two or more Sunday morning services report that the services are significantly different in style.[2] While the report does not give any definitions of what it means by "worship styles," the obvious conclusion is that the rank-and-file of congregations have not given in to the praise-oriented versus traditional schism that the Left wishes to foster upon them. Brethren seem to understand the difference between matters of faith and matters of indifference. They know what Acts 15:28 says: "For it seemed good to the Holy Ghost, and to us, to lay upon you no greater burden than these necessary things."

---

2. Douglas A. Foster & Thomas L. Winter, "The Character of our Congregations," *The Christian Chronicle* 58/2 (February 2001), http://www.christianchronicle. org/0102/p17a1.asp.

THE MAJORITY SHOWS LITTLE CHANGE!

One table of results that should be of great interest concerns changes in worship. The 300 congregations were asked how much their worship patterns or style had changed over the past five years. Quoting from the report: "Interestingly, over half the congregations (51.8 percent) say their worship is basically the same, and another 21 percent say it has changed only a little."[3] Notice the expression of surprise! This was hardly what the surveyors expected to discover. In addition, 20.7 percent say their worship style has changed somewhat, while only 6.5 percent report that the style has changed significantly.[4] Brethren appear to be following Jesus' command in John 4:24: "God is a spirit: and they that worship him must worship him in spirit and in truth."

But there's more. "More controversial worship trends appear to be relatively infrequent among churches of Christ," the report states.[5] This is an understatement, given the results. Of the 300 congregations, 67.5 percent never include dramatic presentations as part of worship. Also, 75.3 percent never use special music by small groups or individuals, and 85.1 percent never use praise teams in worship![6] Now, admittedly this does not consider those who may use these unscriptural practices eventually or those who are considering their use; but it still gives reason for optimism. The Left has, for at least 10 years, made an intensive effort to introduce these practices into the mainstream of churches of Christ. While some high-profile congregations have embraced them completely, the rank-and-file have not. This must be no small area of concern for the "movers and shakers" on the Left, as well as the finding that 97.5 percent of the 300 report they have never used instrumental music![7] Again, it is apparent that brethren realize that Ephesians 5:19 and Colossians 3:16 are inspired commands given to the entire congregation, not praise teams or soloists. Also, they know that instrumental music is unscriptural because it is not authorized (Colossians 3:17).

---

3. Ibid.
4. Ibid.
5. Ibid.
6. Ibid.
7. Ibid.

DOCTRINAL OUTLOOK

One other finding in the study that ought to catch our attention addresses the doctrinal outlook of the members of the 300 congregations surveyed. When asked to describe the majority of adults in each congregation, 20 percent said "very conservative," and 35 percent responded "somewhat conservative." On the other hand, just 35 percent replied "moderate," 9 percent said "somewhat progressive or liberal," and only one congregation said it is "very progressive or liberal."[8]

Of course, this is another instance where definitions are in order. What do the project leaders mean by each term used? When one considers that Douglas Foster had a role in carrying out the survey, one becomes suspicious. Given Foster's track record, one is not predisposed to trust him. Consider:

- In the inaugural issue of *Wineskins,* Foster attributed a quotation from a Baptist minister to David Lipscomb.
- In his book, *Will the Cycle Be Unbroken?* Foster declares that there are no liberals in churches of Christ.
- In the same book, as we have previously shown, Foster slaughters a quotation from G. C. Brewer and attributes beliefs to him he never held.

At any rate, Foster can do little to manipulate raw data. One only wonders if the data contains worse information than has been released.

THE LIBERAL MINORITY

Ponder the tremendous import of the last statistic mentioned. Of the congregations responding, 55 percent consider themselves to at least be "somewhat conservative." Only 9 percent consider themselves to be "liberal"! Of course, the "moderate" 35 percent is a source of concern. But even that may be a positive. Given enough sound teaching, coupled with the excesses of the Left that are already happening, who knows what good may be accomplished? The gospel is still "the power of God unto salvation" (Romans 1:16).

---

8. Ibid.

The historian Thomas C. Reeves is the author of the best-selling biography of John F. Kennedy, *A Question of Character.* In 1996 he penned *The Empty Church: The Suicide of Liberal Christianity.* In it Reeves thoroughly documents how the mainline denominations—American Baptist, Disciples of Christ, Episcopal, Evangelical Lutheran, Presbyterian, Methodist, United Church of Christ—have transformed themselves into bastions of liberalism, both political and religious. He also describes the steady decline of those churches.[9]

Is it not ironic that, at the same time, the Left within the body of Christ wishes to lead us in that direction? One chapter of Reeves' book is titled, "Stuck in the Sixties." Indeed, such is the case with the leaders of the Left. In 1994 I put forth that thesis in *Among the Scholars.* Just two years later, Richard Hughes of Pepperdine wrote *Reviving the Ancient Faith,* in which he devoted three chapters to the sixties, and gushed over the fact that the decade had a profound impact on the Left.

THE CHURCH MUST BE VIGILANT

The majority of brethren do not wish to be led off into spiritual Egypt. Those who conducted the survey have revealed far more than they may have wished to reveal. William Woodson remarked in his book, *Change Agents and Churches of Christ,* that the brotherhood is a "sleeping giant." I thoroughly concur. It is my conviction that the giant is awakening.

Having said that, there must be a constant vigilance to keep from overreacting. In the desire to resist the New Left, some have either wittingly or unwittingly gone to an extreme. This can be summarized by what I call the "Chicken Little" syndrome. You remember Chicken Little of literary fame. She kept on crying, "The sky is falling! The sky is falling!" Even though there was no real danger, she kept it up. Or the "Little Boy Who Cried Wolf" could well describe some in the church. In the story, the boy kept on crying, "Wolf! Wolf!" when there was no wolf. The townspeople eventually paid him no attention. When the wolf really came, they were all slaughtered. There are those within

---

9. Thomas C. Reeves, *The Empty Church: The Suicide of Liberal Christianity* (New York: Free Press, 1996).

the body of Christ who focus on trivialities, lifting them up to "threats to the faith." That has been as destructive as the New Left's assault on the church.

However, we cannot be like the proverbial ostrich and bury our heads in the sand! Danger is real and present; we must be aware and prepare accordingly. All too often when the subject of the New Left is brought up, some say, "Talking about it is going to cause problems! Don't you know it will never happen here? Let's just deal with it when it comes up." What would you think of a pediatrician saying to a young couple with the first newborn: "I know you've heard about childhood diseases—but that's just going to make you upset, and it will make me upset. We'll just deal with then when they happen"? Do you know what my reaction would be? I'd take that baby to another doctor! I want the doctor treating my children to provide preventive medicine; I want my children to be immunized against all childhood diseases. I also want to know everything I can about any dangers my children could face.

WORD INNOCULATION

In like fashion, the Lord's church needs to be "immunized" against the false doctrines of the New Left. It is in this way that brethren will be able to withstand the spiritual diseases Satan uses to infect brethren. The Word of God must be used to provide inoculation for individuals and congregations. Elders must provide the spiritual leadership necessary for congregations to be safe. Preachers must proclaim the whole counsel of God, boldly.

Brethren, keep on preaching the truth! Keep on doing the work of the Lord! You may never know how much good you are doing for the cause of Christ. Remember that Noah saved only himself and his family, yet he is mentioned in Hebrews 11 along with the other heroes of faith. Why? He preached righteousness faithfully, even though only seven heeded his call. Preaching brother, keep on keeping on! Elderships, feed the flock! My brethren, let us all arise and carry the bloodstained banner of Christ to the world!

QUESTIONS FOR DISCUSSION

1. How do you feel about the demise of the Nashville Jubilee? Why?

2. Examine the results of *The Christian Chronicle* survey. Did the results surprise you?

3. Do those on the Left seem surprised that no more congregations are embracing their views? Why?

4. Make a list of things you are doing to help the cause of Christ.